GLOSSA

of

FRENCH LEGAL TERMS

FRENCH-ENGLISH and ENGLISH-FRENCH

compiled by

ALAN S. LINDSEY

HADLEY PAGER INFO

First Edition

ISBN 1-872739-07-5

Copyright© Alan S. Lindsey 1999

Printed and bound in Great Britain by Watkiss Studios Ltd., Biggleswade

HADLEY PAGER INFO
Surrey House, 114 Tilt Road, Cobham, Surrey, KT11 3JH, England

FOREWORD

The Glossary is a completely new compilation providing English translations of over 4000 French legal words and phrases associated with legislation falling within the Civil Code and the Penal Code. In addition to general legal terminology there is a good coverage of terms relating to house purchase and conveyance, leasing and renting of properties, wills and succession law, employment and family matters. Apart from some basic terms Company and Commercial legislation is not covered.

This is a specialist Glossary and is not claimed to be comprehensive. The aim has been to provide a sufficient working range of terminology to allow translation, when used in conjunction with a general French Dictionary, of French legal and official documents.

In preparing the Glossary a wide range of dictionaries and source books has been consulted including the Code Civil and the Code Pénal. It should be noted however that the translations given have no official or statutory basis but represent the most likely English equivalents. It is well known that the meanings of French legal words and phrases can be sensitive to placement and content, and where important legal matters are in question the advice of a bilingual solicitor, lawyer, notaire or avocat should be sought.

The Glossary should prove useful to all students of the French language since many of the words and phrases are used in news and media reports of prominent legal cases, and in particular to students and translators of French legal and official documents.

As with all new compilations, errors can creep in so please notify me if any errors or omissions are found, so that later editions of the Glossary can be suitably amended.

A.S.L.

Abbreviations Used

adj	adjective	*prep*	preposition or prepositional phrase	*admin*	administrative
adv	adverb			*com*	commercial
f	feminine noun			*fig*	figurative
m	masculine noun	*pron*	pronoun	*fin*	financial
inv	invariant	*pp*	past participle	*med*	medical
conj	conjunction	*v*	verb	*mil*	military
pl	plural				

FRENCH-ENGLISH

A

abandon *m* abandonment (of property, children); desertion (of home, wife, husband)
- abandon d'enfant = abandonment of a child
- abandon d'épave = abandonment of a vehicle
- abandon d'incapable = abandonment of a person in need of care
- abandon de créance = composition between debtor and creditor (ie creditor agrees to accept partial in lieu of full payment)
- abandon de famille = desertion of family
- abandon de foyer familial = desertion of the home
- abandon des poursuites = abandonment of action; nolle prosequi
- abandon du domicile conjugal = desertion of the marital home
- biens à l'abandon = ownerless property
- faire abandon de = to relinquish

abandonner *v* desert (to); abandon (to)
- abandonner l'accusation = to drop the charge
- abandonner le domicile conjugal = to desert or abandon the family home
- abandonner un procès = to withdraw an action

absent *m*, **absente** *f* (also *adj*) absentee; missing person

absolution *f* absolution; acquittal; discharge; dismissal (of case, when defendant is considered to have no case to answer)

absoudre *v* dismiss (to); pardon (to); absolve (to)

abus *m* abuse; corrupt practice
- abus de confiance = breach of trust; misuse (of funds, etc)
- abus de mineur = undue influence upon a minor
- abus sexuel = sexual abuse

abusif,-ive *adj* wrongful
- licenciement abusif = unfair dismissal
- poursuite abusive = malicious prosecution

acceptation *f* acceptance; accepting; signing
- acceptation d'une succession = acceptance of an inheritance
- acceptation restreinte = partial acceptance
- acceptation sous réserve = qualified acceptance

accepter *v* accept (to); consent (to)

accident *m* accident
- accident du trajet = accident sustained whilst travelling between home and workplace
- accident du travail = industrial injury; industrial accident

accord *m* agreement; settlement
- accord collectif = collective agreement; joint agreement
- accord complémentaire = additional agreement
- accord irrévocable = binding agreement
- par accord mutuel = both parties agreeing
- se mettre d'accord = to come to an agreement (with someone)
- tomber d'accord = to come to an agreement (with someone)

accroissement *m* increase; growth; accretion (eg of legacy, of rights of survivors by death of co-legatee)

accusation *f* accusation; charge; indictment
- abandonner l'accusation = to drop the charge
- acte d'accusation = indictment
- chambre d'accusation = indictment division of Court of Appeal
- chef d'accusation = count of indictment
- faire les accusations contre quelqu'un = to make charges against someone
- l'accusation (le procureur etc) = the prosecution
- lecture de l'acte d'accusation = arraignment
- mettre en accusation = to indict
- porter / lancer une accusation contre quelqu'un = to lay / bring a charge

against someone
- rédiger l'acte d'accusation = to draw up the indictment
- sur mise en accusation = on indictment

accusatoire *adj* accusatory (procedure)

accusé *m*, **accusée** *f* accused; defendant (in court); prisoner at the bar
- assurer la défense d'un accusé = to conduct the case for the defence

accuser *v* 1 accuse of (to); charge with (to); indict for (to) 2 acknowledge (receipt of) (to)
- accuser quelqu'un d'avoir volé de l'argent = to charge someone of stealing or having stolen money
- tout l'accuse = everything points to his being guilty

achat *m* purchase; buying
- achat ... pour revendre = purchase with the purpose of resale

acheteur *m*, **acheteuse** *f* buyer; purchaser; vendee

acquéreur *m*, **acquéreuse** *f* purchaser; buyer; vendee

acquêt *m* property acquired in common by husband and wife

acquittement *m* acquittal
- verdict d'acquittement = verdict of not guilty

acquitter *v* acquit (to)

acte *m* 1 action; act
- acte délictuel / quasi délictuel = tort
- acte délictueux = tortious act
- actes de violence caractérisés = aggravated assault
- sans acte contraire au droit = without legal wrong

acte *m* 2 deed; title; instrument; legal document
- acte authentique = deed; formal deed (of sale); deed of conveyance
- acte authentique de vente = deed of sale, sale contract; conveyance document
- acte de suscription = superscription to a will
- acte de vente = conveyance document; formal deed (of sale)
- acte définitif = final conveyance document

- acte juridique = legal document or instrument
- acte notarié = notarised deed
- acte sous seing privé = private deed; private agreement; private contract (document signed but not witnessed)
- acte sur papier timbré = notarised deed
- projet d'acte = draft conveyance document

acte *m* 3 record; certificate
- acte de dernière volonté = last will and testament
- acte de l'état civil = birth, marriage or death certificate
- acte de naissance / mariage / décès = birth / marriage / death certificate
- actes publics = public registers
- donner acte de ..., que ... = to give official notice of ..., that ...
- dont acte = duly noted or acknowledged
- dont acte = the following constitutes legal publication

actif *m* assets

action *f* action (at law); lawsuit
- action en contrefaçon = action for infringement of patent
- action en cours = pending action
- action en désaveu de paternité = action for disavowal
- action en diffamation orale = action for slander
- action en dommages et intérêts = action for damages
- action en exécution de contrat = action for specific performance
- action en expropriation = action in expropriation of real property
- action en justice = action
- action en résolution pour inexécution = action for breach of contract
- action en revendication = claim for restitution of property
- action en séparation de corps = action for separation from bed and board
- action judiciaire = action; claim; lawsuit; prosecution
- action juridique / civile = legal / civil action
- action oblique = indirect action
- action par defaut = default action

- action pénale = criminal action
- action pétitoire = claim to property where title is in dispute
- action publique = criminal prosecution
- action rédhibitoire = action seeking recision of a contract
- action résolutoire = action to cancel a lease contract

actionner v sue (to); bring an action against (to)
- actionner quelqu'un en dommages et intérêts = to sue someone for damages

administrateur m administrator
- administrateur judiciaire = receiver (appointed)

administrer v administer
- administrer les biens d'un mineur = to administer the estate of a minor
- administré m, administrée f = citizen; constituent

adoptif,-ive adj adoptive; adopted
- fille adoptive = adopted daughter
- fils adoptif = adopted son
- mère adoptive = adoptive mother; foster mother
- père adoptif = adoptive father; foster father

adoption f adoption

adultère m adultery
- commettre un adultère = to commit adultery
- complice en adultère = co-respondent
- l'adultère est un cas de divorce = adultery is grounds for divorce

adultérin,-e adj adulterine; (child) born of adultery

affacturage m factoring

affactureur m factor

affaire f 1 business; affair; concern; 2 case; lawsuit
- affaire civile = civil action; civil proceedings
- affaire de mœurs = sex case
- être sur une affaire = to be on a case
- l'affaire est portée = the case is conducted
- l'affaire X = the X case
- plaider une affair = to plead a case
- une affaire de vol = a case of theft

affectation f allocation (of a building, etc)

affecter v 1 feign (to); 2 allocate (to); assign (to) 3 affect (to); have an effect on (to)
- domaine affecté d'hypothèques = mortgaged estate; burdened estate

afférent,-e adj relating to; pertaining to
- part afférente à = portion accruing (by right) to
- questions afférentes = related questions
- renseignements afférents à une affaire = information relating to a matter

aggravation f aggravation; worsening
- aggravation de (la) peine = increase in sentence

agréé m counsel formally representing parties before a commercial court

agrément m 1 assent; consent; approval; 2 agreement; 3 pleasure; amusement
- agrément fiscal = tax relief

agression f act of aggression; mugging; assault; attack
- agression sexuelle = sexual attack

aide f aid; assistance; grant
- aide judiciaire = legal aid
- aide juridique; aide juridictionnelle = legal aid
- aide pécuniaire = grant

ajournement m adjournment

ajourner v 1 adjourn (to); put off (to); 2 summon someone to appear (to); subpoena someone (to)

alcootest m 1 Breathalyzer™; 2 breath test
- faire subir un alcootest = to breathalyse / breathalyze
- subir un alcootest = to be breathalysed / breathalyzed

alibi m alibi
- établir / prouver un alibi = to establish an alibi
- produire / fournir un alibi = to produce an alibi

aliénation f 1 alienation; transfer (of rights, property, etc); 2 alienation; estrangement
- aliénation de la chose léguée = prior disposal of the legacy by the testator
- aliénation mentale = derangement of mind; insanity; lunacy

aliéner v 1 alienate (to); part with (to); transfer (to) (eg property, rights); 2 alienate (to); estrange (to)

- aliéner un bien = to dispose of property
aliments *mpl* alimony; maintenance
allégation *f* allegation
allocation *f* benefit; benefits; allocation
- allocation chômage = unemployment
benefit
- allocation de fin de droits = income
support (after unemployment benefit has
ceased)
- allocation de maternité = maternity
benefit
- allocation dégressive = graduated
benefit; diminishing benefit
- allocation logement = housing benefit
- allocation vieillesse = discretionary
retirement pension
- allocations familiales = family benefits
amende *f* fine
- condamnation à une amende =
imposition of a fine
- condamner quelqu'un à une amende =
to impose a fine on someone
- jour-amende *m* = a daily based fine
amiable *adj* amicable
- amiable compositeur = arbitrator
- arranger, régler ou liquider une affaire à
l'amiable = to settle a difference out of
court
- règlement à l'amiable = out-of-court
settlement
- vente à l'amiable = private sale; sale by
private agreement
amovibilité *f* 1 uncertainty of tenure (of
office); 2 removability
amovible *adj* removable; (office) revocable
at pleasure
anéantissement *m* cancellation (eg
contract); destruction; exhaustion;
dejection
année *f* year
- année de référence = relevant year
annexe *f* 1 annexe; extension (to a
building); 2 appendix; annexe; supplement
(to a document); 3 schedule (to a contract)
annulable *adj* voidable; rescindable
annulation *f* annulment; cancellation;
quashing; recision (of writ); setting aside
(eg will); voidance; cancellation (eg of
contract)
- annulation du testament = setting aside

or voidance of will
- annulation pour vice du consentement =
recision
annuler *v* annul (to); cancel (to)
- annuler un contrat pour vice du
consentement = to rescind a contract
antichrèse *f* antichresis; pledging of real
estate (eg as security for a debt)
apologie *f* apology
- faire apologie de = to vindicate; to
justify; to defend (something or
someone)
appel *m* appeal; register; roll call; appeal at
law
- avis d'appel = notice of appeal
- casser un jugement en appel = to quash
a sentence on appeal
- faire appel = to appeal; to lodge an
appeal
- faire appel d'un jugement = to appeal
against a judgment
- juger en appel / sans appel = to judge on
appeal / without appeal
- l'appel est porté = the appeal is carried
- l'appel des causes = reading of the roll
of cases (to be heard)
- la décision de cette cour est sans appel
= there is no appeal from this court
- rejeter un appel = to dismiss an appeal
appelant *m*, **appelante** *f* appellant; plaintiff
in Court of Appeal
- appelant d'un jugement = appellant
against a judgement
appeler *v* call (to)
- appeler d'un jugement = to appeal
against a sentence
- appeler quelqu'un à comparaître comme
témoin = to summon someone as a
witness
appellation *f* designation; appellation
- appellation d'origine = label of origin
- appellation (d'origine) contrôlée =
appellation contrôlée (label guaranteeing
the quality of wine)
application *f* application
- application de / en = pursuant to
apport *m* contribution; investment; supply;
provision
- apport de pièces = deposit of
documents in a suit

- apport effectif = conveyance of actual chattels
- apport en nature = contribution in kind
- apport en numéraire = cash contribution
- apport financier préalable = deposit
- apport personnel = cash deposit; personal financial contribution
- biens d'apport = estate brought in by husband or wife upon marriage
- les apports = goods and property

apposer *v* affix (to) (eg seal, stamp); append (to) (eg signature); insert (to) (clause); place (to); put (to)
- apposer les scellés = to affix the seals (to prevent unlawful entry)
- apposer une clause à un acte = to insert a clause in, add a clause to an act
- faire apposer des scellés sur les biens d'une succession = to have seals placed on the property of an estate

apprenti *m*, **apprentie** *f* apprentice; articled clerk
- apprenti conducteur = learner driver

apprentissage *m* apprenticeship
- contrat d'apprentissage = indenture; articles of apprenticeship

appropriation *f* appropriation

apte *adj* authorized; empowered; fit to; fit for; suited; suitable; apt

aptitude *f* fitness; capacity; aptitude

arbitrage *m* arbitration
- arbitrage en cas de grève = strike arbitration
- arbitrage en matière de salaire = wage arbitration
- commission d'arbitrage = arbitration committee
- porter en arbitrage = to go to / submit to arbitration
- recours à l'arbitrage = appeal to arbitration

arbitral,-e *adj* arbitral
- commission arbitrale = board of referees
- règlement arbitral = settlement by arbitration
- solution arbitrale = settlement by arbitration
- tribunal arbitral = court of arbitration

arbitre *m* arbitrator; arbiter; referee; adjudicator

- arbitre rapporteur = referee (in a commercial suit)
- servir d'arbitre dans un conflit social = to act as an arbiter in an industrial dispute

argument *m* case; argument
- argument décisif = deciding factor
- argument de fait et de droit = contention

arme *f* firearm

arrangement *m* agreement; settlement; arrangement
- arrangement de famille = family settlement (in financial matters)
- sauf arrangement contraire = unless otherwise agreed (or stated)

arrérages *mpl* arrears; monthly instalments (vente en viager)

arrestation *f* arrest
- arrestation illégale = illegal arrest
- en état d'arrestation = under arrest
- ordonner l'arrestation de quelqu'un = to order someone's arrest

arrêt *m* 1 judgement; decision; ruling; 2 arrest
- arrêt de cassation = decision of Cour de Cassation quashing a lesser court's decision
- arrêt de défense = stay of execution
- arrêt de rejet = decision of Cour de Cassation dismissing the appeal
- arrêt infirmatif = decision of Court of Appeal overturning decision of lower court
- arrêt par défaut = judgement by default
- casser un arrêt = to quash a judgement
- faire arrêt sur les appointements = to issue a writ of attachment (on debtor's salary)
- ordre d'arrêt ou mandat d'arrêt = warrant of arrest; warrant for the arrest (of someone)
- rendre un arrêt = to pronounce judgement
- rendre un arrêt confirmatif = to uphold the decision of a lower court

arrêté *m* decision; order; administrative order or decree
- arrêté d'exécution = decree providing for enforcement of a law

- arrêté d'expulsion = deportation order
- arrêté de compte = settlement of an account
- arrêté municipal = bye-law
- prendre un arrêté = to pass a decree

arrêter *v* 1 stop (to); 2 arrest (to); seize (to); 3 fix (to)
- arrêter des poursuites = to stay criminal proceedings
- arrêter les dispositions d'application = to adopt provisions to implement
- être arrêté = to be arrested

arrhes *fpl* deposit
- verser des arrhes = to put down / to pay a deposit

article *m* article; clause (of contract); section

articulation *f* enumeration; setting forth (facts)

articuler *v* enumerate (to); set forth (to) (facts); state (fact) clearly (to)

ascendant,-e *adj*; **ascendant** *m*, **ascendante** *f* 1 ascendant *adj*; 2 ascendant (parent); mother and father

assassinat *m* murder; assassination; premeditated murder
- tentative d'assassinat = attempted murder

assignation *f* serving of a writ, summons or process; writ of summons or subpoena
- assignation à résidence = placing under house arrest
- signifier une assignation à quelqu'un = to serve a summons on someone

assigner *v* summon (to); subpoena (to); cite (to) (a witness); issue a writ (to) (against someone); serve a writ (to) (on someone)
- assigner quelqu'un à résidence = to put someone under house arrest
- assigner quelqu'un en contrefaçon = to bring an action for infringement of patent against someone
- assigner quelqu'un en justice = to issue a writ against someone; to serve a writ on someone

assisté, assistée *adj* & *m,f* in receipt of (state) assistance (person)
- enfants assistés = children in care

association *f* association; society

- association de malfaiteurs = criminal conspiracy

associé *m*, **associée** *f* associate; partner

assujetti *adj* liable; subject; tied; assessed
- assujetti à l'impôt = liable for tax

assurance *f* insurance; assurance
- assurance au tiers = third party insurance
- assurance contre les accidents du travail = employer's liability insurance
- assurance dommage(s)-ouvrage = insurance against building faults
- assurance-incendie = insurance against fire risk
- assurance multirisque = comprehensive insurance
- assurance-vie = life insurance
- police d'assurance = insurance policy
- prime d'assurance = insurance premium

assurer *v* ensure (to); assure (to)
- assurer sa propre défense = to conduct one's own defence
- s'assurer = to get insured; to take out an insurance

assureur *m* insurance agent; insurance company; underwriter
- assureur-conseil = insurance consultant

astreinte *f* constraint; obligation; penalty; daily fine for delay in completing a contract, or in repaying a debt

attaquer *v* attack (to); assail (to); contest (to) (judgement, testimony)
- attaquer quelqu'un en justice = to bring an action against someone

atteinte *f* infringement; breach
- atteinte à l'ordre public = breach of the peace
- atteinte à la propriété = trespass
- atteinte à la sûreté de l'État = betrayal of national security
- atteinte à la vie privée = invasion of privacy
- atteinte au droit = (legal) wrong
- atteinte au droit public = public nuisance
- atteinte aux droits = infringement of rights
- atteinte directe = trespass
- sans acte contraire au droit = without legal wrong

attendu *prep* given or considering (the

circumstances); owing to (events)
- attendu que = whereas; seeing that; since
- les attendus (mpl) (d'un jugement) = the reasons adduced

attentat *m* murder attempt; assassination attempt (political); attack on (a building)
- attentat à la bombe = bomb attack; (terrorist) bombing
- attentat à la pudeur = indecent assault
- attentat aux droits / à la liberté = violation of rights / of liberty
- attentat aux mœurs = offence against public decency
- attentat contre la sûreté de l'État = conspiracy against the security of the State
- un attentat a été perpétré contre M. X = an attempt has been made on the life of Mr. X

atténuation *f* alleviation; mitigation
atténué,-e *adj* attenuated; diminished
- responsabilité atténuée = diminished responsibility

attestation *f* attestation
- attestation du titre = warranty of title
- attestation écrite = written statement; witness statement
- attestation sous serment = affidavit
- attestation sur l'honneur = affidavit

attester *v* attest (to); certify (to); bear witness (to); vouch for (to)
attouchement *m* interfering (sexual); molesting
audience *f* audience; hearing; court hearing; court sitting or session
- audience à huis clos = hearing in camera
- audience de référée = hearing taking place in Chambers
- l'audience est reprise = the case is resumed
- plaider en audience publique = to plead in open court
- plaider en pleine audience = to plead in open court
- registres d'audience = court records
- se présenter à l'audience = to appear in court

audit, auxdit(e)s **(see ledit)** to the aforesaid; to the aforementioned (also at,

in, on, from)
audition *f* audition; examination (of a witness)
- procéder à l'audition d'un témoin = to examine a witness
- nouvelle audition = rehearing

autopsie *f* post-mortem (examination); autopsy
autoriser *v* authorise (to); authorize (to); empower (to)
autorité *f* authority
- autorité parentale = (joint) parental authority (legal)
- être déchu de son autorité paternelle = to lose one's parental rights
- fermé / vendu par autorité de justice = closed / sold by order of the court
- l'autorité de la chose jugée = res judicata
- les agents de l'autorité = the police force

autrui *pron* others; other people
- chose d'autrui = another person's property
- les biens d'autrui = other people's property
- occupation de fait de la maison d'autrui = squatting

avaliser *v* back (to); support (to); endorse (to); guarantee (to)
avant dire droit *m,inv*; **avant faire droit** *m,inv* injunction; interim order
avant-contrat *m* preliminary agreement; preliminary contract
- avant-contrat synallagmatique = preliminary bilateral agreement (eg to buy)

avant-projet *m*; **avant-projets** *mpl* rough draft; preliminary version; draft scheme; draft project; proposed plan; pilot study
avantage *m* 1 advantage; 2 (pl) benefits
- avantages en espèces = cash benefits
- avantages en nature = benefits in kind
- avantages supplémentaires = fringe benefits

avenant *m* amendment; endorsement; rider; additional clause;
- faire un avenant à = to endorse; to amend

avenir *m* writ of summons (from one

counsel to another)

avertissement *m* 1 warning (eg of dismissal); notice 2 demand note *(admin)*
- avertissement sans frais = notice of assessment
- billet d'avertissement = summons to appear before a magistrate
- recevoir un avertissement = to receive a warning; to be admonished

aveu *m* 1 confession; 2 admission; 3 consent
- faire des aveux complets = to make a full confession
- de son propre aveu = on his own admission
- obtenir l'aveu de quelqu'un pour faire quelque chose = to obtain someone's consent to do something

avis *m* opinion; advice
- avis conforme = decision pursuant to
- sauf avis contraire = unless otherwise informed

avocat *m*; **avocate** *f* solicitor; advocate; barrister; counsel; lawyer
- avocat au criminel = criminal lawyer
- avocat commis d'office = duty solicitor
- avocat-conseil = consulting barrister
- avocat d'affaires = business lawyer
- avocat d'entreprise = company lawyer
- avocat de la défense = counsel for the defence or defendant; defending counsel
- avocat de la partie civile = counsel for the plaintiff
- avocat général = counsel for the prosecution; deputy Head of Public Prosecution at a Court of Appeal
- avocat plaidant = court lawyer
- avocat sans cause = briefless barrister
- consultation d'avocat = counsel's opinion
- consulter son avocat = to consult one's lawyer
- l'accusé et son avocat = the accused and his counsel
- l'Ordre des Avocats = Association of Lawyers

avoir *m* property; asset; estate
- doit et avoir = debit and credit

avortement *m* abortion

avoué *m* solicitor; counsel representing

parties before a Court of Appeal only

ayant-cause *m*; **ayants-cause** *mpl* assign; trustee; executor legal successor; successor in title
- les ayants-cause du défunt = the beneficiaries of the deceased

ayant-droit *m*; **ayants-droit** *mpl* rightful claimant or owner; legal successor; assign; assignee; beneficiary; interested party
- ayant-droit à = party entitled to, or eligible for

B

bail *m*; **baux** *mpl* lease; tenancy agreement
- bail à cheptel = lease of livestock
- bail à ferme = farming lease
- bail à loyer = rental lease; house-letting lease
- bail commercial = commercial lease
- bail de droit commun = lease with common rights
- bail emphytéotique = long duration lease (18-99 years)
- donner à bail = to lease (out)
- faire un bail = draw up a lease
- mettre fin au bail = ending / dissolving a lease contract
- passer un bail = to draw up or sign an agreement to lease
- prendre à bail = to lease

bailleur *m*, **bailleresse** *f* landlord; lessor

banc *m* bench; bank
- banc des accusés = dock
- banc des avocats = bar
- banc des magistrats = magistrates' bench
- banc des témoins = witness box
- banc du jury; banc des jurés = jury box

barre *f* bar; rod
- barre (des témoins) = witness box
- barre d'un tribunal = bar of a court of justice
- être appelé à la barre = to be called as a witness
- paraître / comparaître à la barre = to

appear as a witness
- quitter la barre = to stand down; to leave the witness box

barreau *m* bar; rung (of ladder)
- entrer / être admis / reçu au barreau = to be called to the bar
- être derrière les barreaux = to be behind prison bars

bel et bien *adv* entirely; fairly; well and truly

bénéfice *m* profit; advantage; benefit
- bénéfice de discussion = benefit of discussion
- bénéfice de division = right of sureties to go bail each for his own part only
- bénéfice de doute = benefit of the doubt
- il a obtenu un divorce à son bénéfice = he obtained a divorce in his favour
- il perd tout le bénéfice de sa bonne conduite = he loses all the benefits he has gained from his good behaviour

bénéficiaire *m,f* beneficiary; payee (of cheque)

bénéficier *v* profit by (to); benefit from (to)
- bénéficier d'un non-lieu = to be (unconditionally) discharged
- bénéficier de circonstances atténuantes = to be granted mitigating circumstances

bien *m*, **biens** *mpl* 1 good(s); 2 possession(s); property; assets; wealth; goods and chattels
- bien de famille = family estate
- bien-fondé *m*, bien-fondés *mpl* = validity; cogency; merits of case or claim
- biens communes; biens de communauté = communal estate; joint estate of husband and wife
- biens corporel = tangible property
- biens du ménage = household goods
- biens fonciers = landed property
- biens immeubles, biens immobiliers = real estate or property; landed property; realty
- biens meubles, biens mobiliers = personal property or estate; movable property; personalty
- biens personnels = personal property
- biens privés = private property
- biens propres = separate property (of

husband or wife)
- biens publics = public property
- biens sociaux = company assets

bigamie *f* bigamy

bilan *m* 1 appraisal; assessment; 2 balance sheet; statement of accounts
- bilan d'ouverture de liquidation = statement of affairs
- bilan de compétence = competence appraisal
- bilan professional = performance appraisal
- bilan provisoire = provisional estimate
- déposer son bilan = to go into (voluntary) liquidation; to file one's petition (in bankruptcy)
- dresser / établir un bilan = to draw up a balance sheet
- faire le bilan de = to take stock of

blanchiment *m* laundering; bleaching
- blanchiment de l'argent = money laundering

borner *v* **(se)** à restrict to (to); be limited to (to)

bouquet* *m* down payment (of annuity on a property) (see viager)

box *m* **des accusés** dock

branche *f* a point argued (eg of an appeal)

brevet *m* 1 letters patent; patent; (royal) warrant 2 diploma; certificate
- brevet d'invention = patent
- brevet en cours d'agrément = patent pending
- brevet en cours d'homologation = patent pending
- bureau des brevets = patent office

breveté *m*, **brevetée** *f* patentee

bris *m* breaking; wilful damage
- bris de clôture = trespass; breaking-in
- bris de prison = prison breaking
- bris de scellés = breaking of seals

bureau *m* office
- bureau de conservation des hypothèques = mortgage registry; land charges registry
- bureau des hypothèques = mortgage office and land registry
- bureau du cadastre = land registry

C

cadastre *m* land registry; cadastral register; cadastral survey

cadavre *m* corpse; body (of dead person)

cadre* *m* framework
- dans le cadre de = under; within; on the occasion of; as part of

caduc, caduque *adj* null and void; lapsed
- contrat déclaré caduc = agreement declared to have lapsed
- dette caduque = debt barred by the statute of limitation
- devenir caduc = to lapse
- legs caduc = null and void legacy
- rendre caduc = to render null and void; to invalidate

caducité *f* lapsing; lapse of offer; nullity (eg of legacy)

cahier *m* **des charges** specification; schedule of conditions

calomnie *f* calumny; slander; libel

cambriolage *m* housebreaking; burglary; burgling; breaking and entering

capable *adj* capable; fit; entitled; qualified; competent (to do something)

capacité *f* capacity; ability; legal competency
- avoir capacité pour = to be (legally) entitled to
- capacité civile = civil capacity
- capacité contributive = ability to pay tax
- capacité de contracter = contractual capacity
- capacité du testateur = legal competency of testator
- capacité en droit = basic legal qualification
- capacité juridique = legal capacity
- certificat de capacité en droit = certificate permitting holder to practise in certain branches of the legal profession
- priver quelqu'un de capacité légale = to incapacitate someone

capital *m* capital; assets
- capital décès = industrial death benefit

captateur *m*, **captatrice** *f* inveigler
- captateur(-trice) de testament / de succession = legacy hunter

captation *f* captation; inveigling; improper solicitation of a legacy
- captation d'héritage = captation of an inheritance

carambouillage *m*; **carambouille** *f* fraudulent conversion; reselling of unlawfully owned goods; larceny by a baillee

carambouiller *v* convert fraudently (to)

carence *f* deficiency; insolvency; lack of assets; defaulting; shirking one's obligations
- la carence des pouvoirs publics = the inefficiency / indifference of public authorities
- les carences de (défauts) = the inadequacies or shortcomings of
- procès-verbal de carence = statement of insolvency

cas *m* case; instance; circumstance
- au cas où = in the event of; in case
- cas d'homicide / de divorce = murder / divorce case
- cas d'ouverture = grounds for appeal to Cour de Cassation
- cas de force majeure = act of God; cause beyond control
- cas fortuit = fortuitous event
- l'adultère est un cas de divorce = adultery is grounds for divorce
- soumettre un cas au juge = to submit a case to the judge

casier *m* record
- casier fiscal = tax record
- casier judiciaire = police record
- casier judiciaire chargé / vierge = long / clean police record

cassation *f* cassation; annulment; reversal; reversing; quashing; setting aside (of sentence, will, etc)
- Cour de Cassation = Court of Cassation; (final) Court of Appeal

casser* *v* annul (to); quash (to); set aside (to) (sentence, etc) break (to); cashier (to); demote (to)
- faire casser un jugement pour vice de forme = to have a sentence quashed on a technicality

cause *f* case; cause; ground; suit; action

- affaire en cause = case before the court
- appeler une cause = to call (out) a case
- cause à plaider = brief
- cause civile = civil action
- cause criminelle = criminal proceedings
- cause d'une instance = cause of action
- cause directe = proximate cause
- cause sommaire = summary proceedings
- en attendant que notre cause soit appelée = waiting for our case to come up or be called
- en connaissance de cause = knowingly
- entendre une cause = to hear a case
- être chargé d'une cause = to hold a brief
- être en cause = to be party to a suit
- mettre en cause = to implicate; to involve
- plaider sa cause = to plead one's case
- remettre en cause = to challenge

caution *f* security; guarantee; bail bond; surety
- admettre une caution = to grant bail
- caution bonne et solvable = sufficient security
- caution de soumission = bid bond
- caution judiciaire, caution judicatum solvi = security for costs (given by plaintiff in lawsuit)
- caution solidaire = joint and several guarantee
- donner caution pour quelqu'un = to go bail for someone, to be surety for someone
- mettre quelqu'un en liberté sous caution = to let someone out on bail
- se porter caution pour quelqu'un = to stand security or surety for someone
- verser une caution = to pay a deposit, to lay down a security

cédant *m*, **cédante** *f* assignor; grantor; transferor

céder *v* give up (to); surrender (to) (right); transfer (to)
- "bail à céder" = "lease for sale"
- cédant,-e *adj* = assigning
- céder à bail = to lease
- céder ses biens = to make over or transfer one's property
- il a bien voulu céder un bout de terrain = he agreed to part with a plot of ground

- les droits à eux cédés = the rights granted to them

cellule *f* cell; prison cell
censé *adj* considered; supposed
censure *f* censorship; censure; reprimand
censurer *v* censure (to); censor (to)
certificat *m* certificate; bond; warrant
- certificat d'aptitude à la profession d'avocat; CAPA = postgraduate legal qualification (required to practise as a solicitor or barrister)
- certificat d'origine = certificate of origin
- certificat de bonne vie et mœurs = character reference
- certificat d'urbanisme = certificate showing planning status
- certificat de capacité en droit = certicate permitting holder to practise in certain branches of the legal profession
- certificat de travail = work certificate (work record of employee leaving employment)

certification *f* attestation; witnessing; authentication
- certification de signature = attestation of signature

certifier *v* certify (to); attest (to); assure (to)
- certifier une caution = to guarantee a surety
- certifier une signature = to certify or authenticate a signature
- copie certifiée = attested, certified copy
- copie certifiée conforme à l'original = certified copy of the original

cesser *v* cease (to); stop (to)
- cesser ses paiements = to stop or discontinue payment
- cesser tout commerce = to cease trading
- pour faire cesser les poursuites = in order to have the action or proceedings dropped

cessibilité *f* transferability; assignability (eg of estate); negotiability (eg of pension)
cessible *adj* transferable; assignable; negotiable (of pension, etc)
cession *f* transfer; assignment
- acte de cession = deed of transfer; deed of assignment

- cession de biens = assignment of property
- cession d'une créance = transfer of a debt

cession-bail *f* leaseback

cessionnaire *m* transferee; assignee; cessionary; endorser (of cheque)

chambre *f* room; court; division (of a court)
- chambre correctionnelle = magistrates' or district court
- chambre criminelle = court of criminal appeal (in the Cour de Cassation)
- chambre d'accusation = criminal division of court of appeal
- chambre de conseil = Judge's Chambers; magistrates in deliberation after a hearing
- chambre des requêtes = (preliminary) civil appeal court

chantage *m* blackmail
- faire du chantage = to blackmail

chapardage *m* pilfering; theft; scrounging
- menus chapardages = pilfering

charge* *f* charge; load; practice; expense
- charge de la preuve = burden of proof; onus of proof; onus probandi
- charge de notaire = notaire's office and goodwill
- charges = service charges
- charges de famille = dependents
- charges d'un appartement = service charges (payable by tenants)
- charges locatives = maintenance or service charges
- charges publiques = public offices
- charges sociales = social security contributions
- fait de charge = breach of trust
- frais à la charge de ... = costs payable by ...
- il a ses enfants à (sa) charge = he has dependent children
- les charges qui pèsent contre lui = the charges against him
- relever les charges contre quelqu'un = to bring charges against someone
- témoin à charge = witness for the prosecution

charger* *v* charge (to); entrust (to);
- charger quelqu'un de faire quelque chose

= to charge someone with doing something; to instruct someone to do something
- charger quelqu'un de quelque chose = to entrust someone with something

chef *m* head; chief; count
- avoir une terre du chef de sa femme = to own an estate in one's wife's right
- chef d'accusation = count of an indictment; charge
- chef des jurés = foreman of the jury
- le premier chef = the most important count
- répondre à un chef d'accusation = to answer a charge

cheptel *m* livestock; contract of agistment
- bail à cheptel = lease of livestock
- cheptel mort = farm equipment leased
- cheptel vif = livestock leased

chicane* *f* chicanery; pettifoggery; quibbling

chômage *m* unemployment
- allocation chômage = unemployment benefit
- assurance chômage = compulsory unemployment insurance
- chômage partiel = short-time working
- être au chômage = to be unemployed; to be jobless
- indemnité de chômage = unemployment benefit
- mettre au chômage technique = to lay off
- travailleurs mis au chômage technique = laid off workers

chômeur *m*, **chômeuse** *f* unemployed person

chose *f* thing
- la chose jugée = the res judicata; the final decision

ci-après *adv* below; hereinafter

ci-inclus *adj* enclosed; herewith

ci-joint *adj* herewith; attached
- les pièces ci-jointes = the documents herewith

circonstance *f* circumstance; incident; event; occasion
- circonstances aggravantes = aggravating circumstances
- circonstances atténuantes = mitigating

or extenuating circumstances
- circonstances et dépendances = appurtenances

citation *f* summons; writ of summons; citation; quotation
- citation à comparaître = summons to appear (to accused); subpoena (a witness)

citer *v* cite (to); summon (to); subpoena (to) (a witness)

civil *m & adj* civilian; civil *adj*
- policier en civil = plain-clothes policeman; policeman in plain clothes
- le civil = private life
- droit civil = civil law
- poursuivre quelqu'un au civil = to sue someone in the civil courts

civilement *adv* civilly
- enterré civilement = to be buried without religious ceremony
- être civilement responsable = to be legally responsible
- poursuivre quelqu'un civilement = to take civil action against someone; to sue someone in the (civil) courts
- se marier civilement = to contract a civil marriage; to be married at a registry office

clause *f* clause; term; article; provision; stipulation
- clause abusive = unfair term or clause
- clause additionnelle = additional clause, rider
- clause aléatoire = aleatory or chance-dependent clause
- clause compromissoire = arbitration clause
- clause conditionnelle = conditional clause
- clause de non-responsabilité = non-liability clause; exemption clause
- clause de style = standard or set clause; formal clause
- clause dérogatoire = escape clause; overriding clause
- clause facultative = optional clause
- clause léonine = one-sided clause
- clause pénale = penalty clause
- clause résolutoire = resolutive clause
- clause restrictive = saving clause

- clause suspensive = suspensive or let-out clause

coaction *f* coercion; compulsion

coadministrateur *m*, **coadministratrice** *f* co-trustee; co-director

coauteur *m* collaborator; co-author; accomplice

codétenteur *m*, **codétentrice** *f* joint holder
- codétenteur / codétentrice d'un héritage = joint heir / heiress

code *m* code
- code civil = civil code; common law
- code du travail (de procédure) = labour regulations or laws
- code pénal = penal code; criminal law
- code postal = postcode
- le code maritime / de commerce = maritime / commercial law

codéfendeur *m* co-defendant; co-respondant

codicillaire *adj* codicillary

codicille *m* codicil

codifier *v* codify (to) (laws, etc)

cohabitation *f* cohabitation; living with somebody

cohabiter *v* cohabit (to); live together (to)

collatéral *m*, **collatéraux** *mpl* brother(s) and sister(s); collateral; relative(s)

collocation *f* order of priority of creditors (in a bankruptcy) and sum due to them
- collocation utile = ranking (of creditors)

commandement *m* command; summons to pay; order to pay
- agir en vertu d'un commandement = to act as agent (in a purchase); to act under instructions

commencement *m* beginning; commencement
- commencement d'exécution = attempt
- commencement de preuve par écrit = prima facie evidence

commettant *m* principal (to a contract) vendor or buyer (when represented by an agent)
- commettant et agent = principal and agent

commettre *v* commit (to) (crime, etc); appoint (to)
- avocat commis d'office = barrister appointed by the court

compétent

- commettre un arbitre = to nominate or appoint an arbitrator

comminatoire *adj* threatening (letter); comminatory (decree); appointing a penalty for non-compliance

commissaire *m* commissioner
- commissaire de police = police superintendent
- commissaire-priseur = auctioneer

commission *f* charge; warrant; committee; commission
- avoir la commission de faire quelque chose = to be empowered or commissioned to do something
- commission d'arbitrage = arbitration committee
- commission d'enquête = fact-finding commission; board of enquiry
- commission paritaire = joint consultative committee
- commission rogatoire = rogatory commission
- commission temporaire = ad hoc committee

commun,-e *adj* common; collaborative
- biens communes = communal estate; joint estate of husband and wife
- époux communs en biens = couple jointly owning property through marriage

communauté *f* community; commonalty
- biens de communauté = communal estate; joint estate of husband and wife
- communauté conventionnelle = community by agreement (between husband and wife)
- communauté de biens = joint estate
- communauté légale = joint ownership of property on marriage
- communauté réduite aux acquêts = joint ownership of property on marriage
- communauté urbaine = urban district
- en communauté = joint ownership (of property)
- régime de la communauté des biens = husband's and wife's joint estate
- se marier sous le régime de la communauté = to marry on terms of joint ownership of property

commutatif,-ive *adj* commutative (eg contract)

commutation *f* 1 commutation (of penalty); 2 switching

comparaître *v* appear before a court of justice (to)
- citation à comparaître = summons to appear
- comparaître en justice = to appear before a court of justice
- comparaître par avocat = to be represented by counsel
- defaut de comparaître = default / failure to appear
- être appelé à comparaître = to be summoned to appear
- refus de comparaître = refusal to appear

comparution *f* appearance (before the court)
- mandat de comparution = summons
- non-comparution = non-appearance; default
- par défaut de comparution = for want of prosecution

compensation *f* compensation; settlement per contra
- chambre de compensation = clearing house
- compensation des dépens = division / sharing of the costs

compenser *v* compensate (to); counterbalance (to); set off (to) (eg debts); clear (to) (cheques)

compétence *f* competence; competency; jurisdiction; powers (of court, etc)
- c'est de la compétence de ce tribunal = it's within the competence of this court
- compétence en appel = appellate jurisdiction
- compétence en matière civile / pénale = civil / criminal jurisdiction
- être en dehors de la compétence du tribunal = to fall outside the court's jurisdiction
- hors de la compétence de = ultra vires
- relever de la compétence d'un tribunal = to fall within a court's jurisdiction

compétent,-e *adj* competent; capable; relevant
- adressez-vous à l'autorité compétente = apply to the authority concerned
- être compétent pour faire quelque chose

18

= to have jurisdiction to do something

complice *adj & m,f* 1 accomplice;
2 co-respondent
- complice en adultère = co-respondent
- complice par instigation / par assistance = accessory before / after the fact
- être complice de quelqu'un = to be someone's accomplice; to be in collusion with someone; to aid and abet

complicité *f* complicity; aiding and abetting
- agir en complicité avec quelqu'un = to act in complicity with someone

complot *m* conspiracy; plot

comploter *v* conspire (to); plot (to)

compromis *m* compromise; arrangement
- compromis de vente = bilateral agreement to sell / buy; preliminary contract to buy
- mettre une affaire en compromis = to submit an affair for arbitration

comptable *m,f* accountant

compte *m* count; counting; account (eg bank); statement
- arrêté de compte = settlement of account
- compte courant conjoint = joint current account

compte rendu *m* report; progress report (eg of building work)
- faire le compte rendu de = to report on

concerner *v* concern (to)
- en / pour ce qui concerne = by way of; in respect of; concerning; in regard to; regarding

conciliation *f* conciliation; reconciliation
- ordonnance de non-conciliation = (in divorce suit) order pendente lite regarding wife's domicile, alimony and custody of children

conciliatoire *adj* conciliatory

concilier *v* reconcile (to); conciliate (to)

conclure *v* conclude (to)
- conclure contre quelqu'un = to convict someone
- conclure sa plaidoirie = to rest one's case
- j'en conclus que = I therefore conclude that
- le jury a conclu au suicide = the jury returned a verdict of suicide

- les juges ont conclu à l'acquittement = the judges decided on an acquittal
- on vous demande de conclure = will you please bring your discussion to a close

conclusion *f* conclusion; findings
- conclusions = findings; conclusions (jury)
- conclusions = pleadings; submissions (petitioner, applicant)
- conclusions = summing-up; statement of claim (barrister)
- déposer des conclusions auprès d'un tribunal = to file submissions with a court

concordant,-e *adj* which agree; which are in agreement; corroborating

concours *m* **d'infractions** combination of offences

concubin *m*, **concubine** *f* common law husband / wife; cohabitant; co-habitee

concubinage *m* common-law marriage; common-law couple; cohabitation
- ils vivent en concubinage = they live together as husband and wife; they cohabit
- les enfants issus du concubinage = children born to a cohabiting couple

condamnation* *f* conviction; judgement; sentence; sentencing
- condamnation à cinq ans de prison = five year prison sentence
- condamnation à mort = death sentence
- condamnation à perpétuité = life sentence
- condamnation à une amende = imposition of a fine
- condamnation à vie = life sentence
- condamnation aux dépens = order to pay costs
- condamnation par défaut ou par contumace = decree by default or in one's absence
- purger un condamnation = to serve one's sentence

condamner *v* sentence (to); convict (to)
- condamné pour = convicted of
- condamner à une peine = to sentence
- condamner quelqu'un à une amende = to impose a fine on someone
- condamner quelqu'un par défaut ou par

contumace = to sentence someone in absentia
- être condamné aux dépens = to be ordered to pay costs

condition *f* condition; requirement; stipulation; term of contract
- condition particulière = specific / special condition
- condition résolutoire = resolutive condition; (see résolutoire)
- condition suspensive = suspensive / conditional term
- conditions d'un contrat = terms, articles of a contract
- conditions de paiement = terms of payment
- conditions générales = general conditions / terms
- dans les conditions = as provided
- dans les conditions et selon = as provided and in accordance with

conduite *f* driving
- conduite dangereuse = dangerous driving; reckless driving
- conduite en état d'ivresse = drunken driving

confection* *f* making; construction; preparation; drawing up (of deed, will); compilation (of inventory)
- confection du testament = drawing up of will

confirmer *v* confirm (to); affirm (to)
- confirmer la déposition de quelqu'un = to corroborate someone's testimony
- confirmer un jugement = to affirm; to confirm

confiscation *f* confiscation; forfeiture

confisquer *v* confiscate (to); seize (to) (goods, property)

conflit *m* conflict; clash; dispute
- conflit d'intérêts = conflict of interests
- conflit de compétence = conflict of jurisdiction
- conflit de juridiction = conflict of jurisdiction
- conflit de lois = conflict of laws
- conflit du travail = industrial dispute
- règles de conflit = rules determining which court is competent

conformer *v* conform (to); comply (to)

- conforme au droit = in accordance with the law

confusion *f* confusion
- avec confusion des peines = with concurrency of sentences
- confusion de part; confusion de paternité = doubt over paternity
- confusion des dettes = extinguishment of debts (through one creditor or debtor succeeding to the estate of the other)
- confusion des pouvoirs = non-separation of powers

congé *m* 1 leave; permission; 2 notice of dismissal, discharge or non-continuance
- congé à salaire plein = leave on full-pay
- congé annuel = annual leave
- congé (de) maladie = sick leave
- congé (de) maternité = maternity leave
- congé sabbatique = sabbatical leave
- congé sans traitement = unpaid leave
- congés payés = holidays with pay; paid holiday
- donner congé à quelqu'un = to give someone notice (of dismissal)
- donner congé à un bailleur = to give a lessor notice that tenant is not renewing the lease
- donner congé à un locataire = to give a tenant notice to quit
- donner congé un mois d'avance = to give a month's notice
- être en congé = to be on leave; to be on holiday
- la durée du congé est trois mois = the notice to discontinue (the lease) is three months

congédier *v* dismiss (to)

conjoint,-e *adj*; **conjoint** *m* 1 joint; conjoined; 2 spouse; husband or wife
- compte courant conjoint = joint current account
- conjoint fautif = offending spouse
- conjoint survivant = surviving husband / wife
- légataires conjoints = co-legatees
- legs conjoint = joint legacy
- les conjoints = husband and wife
- les (futurs) conjoints = the engaged couple; the bride and groom

conjointement *adv* jointly

- agir conjointement avec quelqu'un = to act in conjunction with someone
- conjointement avec = together with
- conjointement et solidairement = jointly and severally

connaître de *v* take cognizance of (to)
- connaître d'un différend = to hear and determine a dispute
- connaître d'un grief = to deal with a grievance

consécutif,-ive *adj* consecutive; consequential

conseil *m* 1 counseller; counsel; 2 council; board; committee; meeting
- conseil d'enquête = court of enquiry
- conseil de famille = board of guardians
- conseil des prud'hommes = industrial arbitration court
- conseil en propriété industrielle = patent lawyer
- conseil juridique = legal expert / adviser
- Conseil supérieur de l'audiovisuel (CSA) = TV body which monitors broadcasting
- Conseil supérieur de la magistrature = High Council for the Judiciary
- tenir conseil = to hold a meeting; to deliberate

conseiller *m* **conseillère** *f* adviser; counsellor; judge
- conseiller à la Cour d'Appel (ou Cour de Cassation) = judge of appeal
- conseiller juridique; conseillère juridique = legal adviser; lawyer
- conseiller référendaire = assistant judge in the Cour de Cassation

consensuel,-elle *adj* consensual (eg contract)

consentant,-e *adj* consenting; willing

consentement *m* consent
- divorce par consentement mutuel = divorce by mutual consent
- donner / accorder son consentement = to give one's consent

conservateur *m* District Land Registrar

conservation *f* **des hypothèques** land registry

considérer *v* consider (to); study (to)
- considérant que = whereas
- vous êtes considéré comme responsable = you are held to be liable

consignataire *m* depositary; trustee; consignee

consignation *f* deposit (of money); consignment
- faire une consignation à greffe = to deposit a sum with the registrar

constat *m* certified report ; official statement (on accident etc) (spoken or written)
- constat à l'amiable = jointly agreed statement for insurance purposes
- constat d'accident = accident report
- constat d'huissier = affidavit made by a process-server; official report by bailiff

constatation *f* 1 verification; establish - ment (eg of fact); 2 certified statement
- constatation d'identité = proof of identity
- constatation de décès = proof of death
- constatation de paternité = proof of paternity
- constatations d'une enquête = findings of an enquiry
- constatations d'usage = routine investigations

constater *v* establish (to); verify (to); certify (to) (eg a death)

constituant *m* settlor; grantor (of annuity or dowry); constituent

constituer *v* constitute (to); settle (to); appoint (to)
- constituer le jury = to empanel the jury
- constituer quelqu'un procureur = to confer someone with power of attorney; to make someone one's proxy
- constituer quelqu'un son héritier = to make someone one's heir
- constituer un avocat = to brief or retain a solicitor / lawyer
- constituer une dot / une rente à quelqu'un = to settle a dowry / an annuity on someone
- se constituer partie civile = to bring a civil action for damages (in a criminal case)
- se constituer prisonnier = to give oneself up
- se constituer témoin = to come forward as witness

constitution* *f* constitution; appointing;

setting-up
* constitution d'avocat = retaining a
lawyer
* constitution d'un dossier d'inscription =
preparing an application
* constitution de partie civil = instituting a
civil action for damages
construction *f* building; construction
* prêt à la construction = building loan
* vice de construction = construction fault
or defect (building)
contentieux,-ieuse *adj*; **contentieux** *m*
1 contentious; 2 matters in dispute;
litigation; 3 legal department
* bureau du contentieux = legal
department (eg of bank, administration)
* contentieux commercial = commercial
litigation
contestation *f* contestation; dispute
* contestation de paternité = contestation
of paternity
contester *v* contest (to) (eg inheritance,
right, competence); take issue (to); protest
(to)
contractant,-e *adj*; **contractant** *m*;
contractante *f* 1 contracting;
2 contracting party
contradiction *f* contradiction; opposition
* être en contradiction avec les faits = to
be at variance with the facts
* leurs témoignages sont en contradiction
= their testimonies contradict each other
* témoignage qui défie toute contradiction
= incontrovertible evidence
contradictoire *adj* 1 contradictory;
conflicting; 2 after due hearing of the
parties (eg of judgement)
* contradictoirement (adv) = after due
hearing of the parties
* examen contradictoire = cross-
examination
* jugement contradictoire = judgement
given after due hearing of the parties
contraindre *v* constrain (to); restrain (to);
compel (to); force (to)
* contraindre par voie de justice = to
constrain by law (to pay debt)
* contraindre quelqu'un en justice = to
bring an action against someone
contrainte *f* 1 constraint; restraint;

2 compulsion; duress
* contrainte par corps = civil
imprisonment
* la contrainte par saisie de biens = to
distrain (on someone)
* porteur de contrainte = writ server;
bailiff
* sous la contrainte = under duress
contrat *m* contract; agreement; deed
* confirmer un contrat = to affirm a
contract
* contrat à titre gratuit = gratuitous
contract
* contrat à titre onéreux = onerous
contract
* contrat aléatoire = aleatory contract
* contrat clé en main = turnkey contract
* contrat conclu dans les conditions
normales du commerce = arm's length
agreement
* contrat consensuel = consensual
contract (as opposed to contrat solennel)
* contrat d'adhésion = standard contract
* contrat d'apprentissage = indenture;
articles of apprenticeship
* contrat d'assurance = insurance policy
* contrat d'entreprise = business contract;
company contract
* contrat de bail = lease contract
* contrat de consultant = consulting
agreement
* contrat de distribution = distributor
agreement
* contrat de licence = licence agreement
* contrat de location = rent agreement;
tenancy agreement
* contrat de location-vente = hire
purchase contract
* contrat de louage d'ouvrage = contract
for services
* contrat de mariage = pre-marital
agreement; marriage settlement
* contrat de représentation = agency
agreement
* contrat de reservation = reservation
contract (eg for purchase of property
under construction)
* contrat de société = deed or articles of
partnership
* contrat de travail = contract of

employment
- contrat écrit = written contract
- contrat solennel = formal contract (as opposed to contrat consensuel)
- contrat synallagmatique = bilateral contract; contract in which both parties are equally bound
- contrat translatif = conveyance
- contrat unilatéral = contract creating only rights for one party and only duties for the other
- éteindre un contrat = to discharge a contract
- exécuter un contrat = to carry out a contract
- inexécution d'un contrat = non-completion of a contract
- interpréter les termes d'un contrat = to construe the terms of a contract
- objet du contrat = purpose of the contract
- passer un contrat avec quelqu'un = to enter into an agreement with someone; to sign a contract with someone
- quasi-contrat = quasi-contract; implied contract; virtual contract
- résilier un contrat = to cancel a contract
- respecter les termes d'un contrat = to comply with a contract; to perform a contract
- rupture de contrat = breach of contract

contravention *f* minor offence; breach; infringement; fine; parking fine; parking ticket
- donner / filer une contravention à quelqu'un = to issue a parking ticket to someone; to fine someone
- dresser contravention à quelqu'un = to issue a parking ticket to someone; to fine someone
- être en contravention à = to be in contravention of / infraction of

contre-lettre *f* counter-deed; defeasance
contrefaçon *f* forgery; counterfeiting; infringement
- poursuivre la contrefaçon = to take action for infringement of a patent
- procès en contrefaçon = action for infringement

contrefacteur *m* forger; counterfeiter

copie

contrefaire *v* forge (to); counterfeit (to)
contrepartie *f* 1 compensation; consideration; 2 other party (of transaction); 3 counterpart; duplicate
- en contrepartie = in compensation
- moyennant contrepartie valable = for a good and valuable consideration

contreseing *m* countersignature
- avoir le contreseing de quelqu'un = to be authorized to sign for someone

contrevenant,-e *adj*; **contrevenant** *m,* **contrevenante** *f* 1 offending; 2 offender
contrevenir *v* contravene (to)
- contrevenir aux règlements = to contravene the regulations

contributif,-ive *adj* contributory; contributive
contumace *adj & m,f* 1 in default; defaulting; 2 defaulter; absconder
- par contumace = in absentia; in his / her absence

convenir *v* 1 suit (to); 2 agree (to)
- il est convenu = it is understood; it is agreed

convention *f* agreement
- conventions = articles, clauses (of a deed)
- convention en écrit; convention par écrit = agreement in writing
- projet de convention = draft agreement
- sauf convention contraire = unless otherwise agreed

conventionnel,-elle *adj* conventional; contractual (eg deed, clause)
- communauté conventionnelle = community by agreement (between husband and wife)

convocation *f* convocation; summons; notification to attend (written)
coobligé *m*; **coobligée** *f* co-obligant; co-obligor; joint debtor
copartager *v* (une succession) succeed jointly (to); coparcener (to be); co-heir(ess) (to be)
coparticipant,-e *adj & m,f* 1 in copartnership; partner in joint account; 2 copartner
coparticipation *f* copartnership
- coparticipation aux bénéfices = profit-sharing

copie *f* copy

23

copier *v* copy (to); make a copy of (to)
copropriété *f* co-ownership; joint
ownership
- immeuble en copropriété = block of
  flats; a condominium
- logement en copropriété = apartment
  block
- règlements de copropriété = rules of
  condominium
corps *m* body
- corps de métier = trade association or
  guild
- corps de preuves = body of evidence
- corps du délit = corpus delicti
- corps du Droit Civil = corpus of civil law
- le corps législatif = legislative body
- le corps médical = the medical
  profession
correctionnel,-elle *adj*; **correctionnelle** *f*
1 (of tribunal) magistrates court;
2 magistrates court; court of summary
jurisdiction
- délit correctionnel = minor offence
- peine correctionnelle = penalty (imposed
  by court)
- tribunal (de police) correctionnel =
  magistrates court
corrompre *v* bribe (to); corrupt (to)
- corrompre les juges = to bribe the
  judges
- essayer de corrompre un témoin = to try
  to suborn a witness; to tamper with a
  witness
corruption *f* bribery; corruption
- corruption de témoins = suborning /
  bribing of witnesses
cotisation *f* contribution; subscription; fee;
dues
- cotisation patronale = employer's share
- cotisations à la sécurité sociale = social
  security contributions
cotiser *v* contribute (to)
coup *m* blow; knock
- coups et blessures = assault and
  battery; aggravated assuault
- être sous le coup d'un arrêté d'expulsion
  = to be under a deportation order
coupable *adj & m,f* 1 guilty; 2 culprit;
delinquent
- avec intention coupable = with guilty

intent
- négligence coupable; négligence
  criminelle = criminal negligence
- non coupable = not guilty
- reconnaître quelqu'un coupable = to find
  someone guilty
cour *f* court
- Cour d'appel = Court of Appeal
- Cour d'assises = criminal court
- Cour d'assises des mineurs = juvenile
  court
- Cour de Cassation = Court of Cassation;
  Court of Appeal (final)
- Cour de justice = Court of Justice
- Cour européenne de justice = European
  Court of Justice
- cour martiale = court martial
- Messieurs, la Cour! = all rise (in court)
créance *f* debt; claim (financial); letter of
credit
- créance douteuse = bad debt
- créance garantie = secured debt
- créance hypothécaire = mortgage loan
- créance irrécouvrable = bad debt
- créances à recouvrer = outstanding
  debts
- mauvaises créances ou créances
  véreuses = bad debts
- nos créances = moneys owed to us
créancier *m*, **créancière** *f* creditor
crime *m* crime; felony; indictable offence;
murder
- crime (à motif) sexuel = sex murder or
  sex crime
- crime contre les mœurs = sexual
  offence
- crime crapuleux = murder for money
- crime d'incendie = arson
- crime de faux = forgery
- crime de sang = murder
- crime passionnel = crime of passion;
  crime passionnel
- l'arme du crime = the murder weapon
- la victime du crime = the murder victim
criminaliser *v* criminalize (to)
- criminaliser une cause = to refer a case
  to a criminal court (from a civil court)
criminalité *f* criminality; criminal nature (of
an act); crime; delinquency
- criminalité juvénile = juvenile

delinquency
criminel,-elle *adj & m,f* 1 criminal;
2 murderer / murderess; criminal
▪ avocat au criminel = criminal lawyer
▪ poursuivre quelqu'un au criminel = to
take criminal proceedings against
someone
criminellement *adv* criminally
cumul *m* plurality; accumulation
▪ avec cumul de peines = sentences to
run consecutively
▪ cumul d'infractions = combination of
offences
cumulativement *adv* by accumulation;
cumulatively
▪ purger des peines cumulativement = to
serve one's sentences consecutively
cumuler *v* cumulate (to); accumulate (to)
▪ cumuler deux traitments = to draw two
separate salaries
▪ les intérêts cumulés = accrued interests
curatelle *f* legal guardianship
▪ placer quelqu'un en curatelle = to place
someone under guardianship

D

défaillant,-e *adj* 1 failing; faltering;
2 defaulting
défendeur *m*, **défenderesse** *f* defendant;
respondent
▪ défendeur en appel = respondent
dame *f* lady
▪ la dame Dupont = Mrs. Dupont;
Madame Dupont (in court)
▪ les dames du Sacré-Cœur = the religious
of the Sacred Heart
date *f* date
▪ à la date prescrite = on the prescribed
date
▪ date authentique = certified date
▪ date d'achèvement = completion date
▪ date d'échéance = date of maturity
▪ date d'entrée en vigueur = effective
date; date of coming into force
▪ prendre effet à la date de = to take

effect from; to be operative from
dation *f* dation; legal act of giving or
conferring (guardianship, etc)
▪ dation en paiement = dation in payment;
payment in kind
de cujus *m* the deceased
débat *m* discussion; debate
▪ débats = proceedings; debates
▪ débats à huis clos = hearing in camera
▪ les débats d'une affaire criminelle = trial
or hearing of a criminal case
▪ débat intérieur = inner struggle
débiteur,-trice *adj & m,f* 1 *adj* debit;
debtor; 2 debtor
▪ avoir un compte débiteur = to be
overdrawn
▪ débiteur-gagiste *m* = lienee
▪ débiteur hypothécaire *m* = mortgager;
morgage debtor
▪ débiteur insolvable = insolvent debtor;
insolvent
▪ solde de banque débiteur = debit
balance; overdraft
débouté *m* nonsuit
déboutement *m* nonsuit; nonsuiting
débouter *v* nonsuit (to); dismiss / reject a
suit (to)
▪ débouter quelqu'un de sa plainte = to
nonsuit a plaintiff
▪ être débouté de sa demande = to be
ruled out of court; to be unsuited; to
have no case
décéder *v* die (to); decease (to)
▪ décéder ab intestat = to die intestate
▪ prédécéder = to predecease; to die first
décerner *v* 1 decree (to); order (to); issue
(to); 2 award (to); bestow (to)
▪ décerner un mandat d'arrêt contre
quelqu'un = to issue a writ or warrant
for the arrest of someone
décès *m* decease; death (natural)
▪ capital décès = industrial death benefit
▪ prédécès *m* = predecease
décharge* *f* discharge; discharging;
unloading
▪ il faut dire à sa décharge que ... = it
must be said in his defence that ...
▪ témoignage à votre décharge = evidence
that exonerates you
▪ témoin à décharge = witness for the

25

défaut

defence
décharger* *v* unload (to); discharge (to)
- décharger quelqu'un d'une dette = to release someone from a debt
- décharger ses cautions = to surrender to one's bail
- décharger un accusé = to discharge an accused person
- failli déchargé = discharged bankrupt
- failli non-déchargé = undischarged bankrupt

déchéance *f* fall; decline; forfeiture (of rights, etc); loss
- déchéance d'une police = expiration of a policy
- déchéance de l'autorité parentale = loss of parental rights
- déchéance de la propriété littéraire = lapse of copyright
- déchéance de la puissance paternelle = loss of parental rights
- déchéance de nationalité = loss or withdrawal of nationality
- déchéance des droits = forfeiture of rights

déchu,-e *adj* [*p.p* of **déchoir**] fallen
- être déchu de ses droits = to be deprived of one's rights; to forfeit one's rights
- police déchue = expired policy

décision *f* decision; ruling
- décision d'un jury = verdict
- décision d'un tribunal = ruling
- décision exécutoire = binding decision
- par décision judiciaire = by court order

déclarant *m*, **déclarante** *f* informant; avowant

déclaratif,-ive *adj* declaratory (act, statute); declarative

déclaration *f* declaration; statement; admission; registration; notification
- déclaration d'impôts = statement of income; tax declaration; tax return
- déclaration de faillite = declaration of bankruptcy
- déclaration sous serment = affidavit
- faire une déclaration d'une accident = to report an accident (to police)
- fausse déclaration = misrepresentation; mis-statement

- la déclaration du jury = the finding of the jury

déclaratoire *adj* declaratory

déclarer* *v* declare (to); announce (to); state (to); admit (to); confess to (to)
- déclarer quelqu'un coupable / innocent = to find someone guilty / innocent
- déclarer quelqu'un en faillite = to declare someone bankrupt
- déclarer un enfant à la mairie = to register a (new-born) child at the town hall
- se déclarer incompétent = to decline a jurisdiction

décliner *v* 1 decline (to); turn down (to); refuse (to); 2 state (to)
- décliner son identité = to give one's personal details
- décliner une jurisdiction = to refuse to acknowledge a jurisdiction
- décliner vos nom, prénoms, titre et qualités = state your name, forenames, qualifications and status

déconfiture *f* insolvency; bankruptcy; failure
- tomber en déconfiture = to fail to meet one's liabilities; to default

décret *m* decree; order in council; ordinance; writ; warrant of arrest

décréter *v* decree (to); order (to)

dédit *m* forfeit; penalty (for breaking a contract, etc)
- clause de dédit = forfeit clause

dédommagement *m* compensation
- réclamer un dédommagement = to claim compensation

dédommager *v* compensate (to)

défaillance *f* 1 extinction; lapse; fainting; 2 default(ing); non-appearance
- défaillance de mémoire = lapse of memory

défaut *m* default; flaw; fault; absence; deficiency
- défaut caché = latent / hidden defect
- défaut-congé *m* = dismissal of case through non-appearance
- défaut d'entretien = lack of maintenance or upkeep
- défaut de comparution = default; non-appearance; failure to appear

- défaut de paiement = default in payment; non-payment
- faire défaut = to fail to appear; to default; to make default
- jugement par défaut = judgement by default

défendeur *v*, **défenderesse** *f* defendant

défendre *v* 1 defend (to); stand up for (to); 2 forbid (to); prohibit (to)
- agir à son corps défendant = to act under duress or coercion
- tuer quelqu'un à son corps défendant = to kill someone in self-defence

défense *f* defence
- assurer la défense d'un accusé = to conduct the case for the defence
- avocat de la défense = counsel for the defence
- cas de légitime défense = case of self-defence
- défense au contraire = counter claim
- défense au fond = defence
- légitime défense = self-defence
- moyen de défense = ground for defence
- présenter la défense = to put the case for the defence

défenseur *m* defender; advocate; counsel for the defence

déférer *v* submit (to); refer (to) (case to court); bring (to) (case to court); distribute (to)
- déféré au juge = brought before the judge
- déférer le serment à quelqu'un = to administer the oath to someone; to swear (witness); to swear in (jury)
- déférer une succession = to distribute an inheritance

défunt *m* deceased; defunct

dégâts *mpl* damage
- dégâts des eaux = water damage; flood damage
- évaluer les dégâts = to assess the damage

dégradation *f* degradation; debasement
- dégradation civique = loss of civil rights
- les dégradations = damage (eg to a building)

dégrèvement *m* 1 relief; exemption (from tax); 2 reduction; abatement (of tax); 3 disencumbrance (of a mortgage)
- dégrèvement fiscal = tax relief; tax allowance

délai *m* delay; time-limit; deadline; waiting period; extension of time
- dans les délais prescrits, réglementaires, voulus = within the prescibed, required time
- délai congé = period of notice
- délai de carence = grace period; waiting period (for social security benefit)
- délai de droit commun = ordinary time limitation
- délai de forclusion = time limit
- délai de grâce = respite of debt; grace period; extension of time
- délai de livraison = delivery date; delivery time; terms of delivery
- délai de préavis = notice
- délai de réflexion = time for consideration; cooling-off time
- délai expiré = after the deadline
- délai fixé = fixed time limit
- délai imparti = the time allowed
- obtenir un délai = to get a time extension for payment

délaissement *m* abandonment; desertion; neglect; state of neglect ; relinquishment or renunciation (of a right)
- délaissement d'un mineur = abandonment of a minor
- délaissement par hypothèque = abandonment of mortgaged property

délaisser *v* abandon (to); quit (to); neglect (to); relinquish (to) (right)
- délaisser des poursuites = to abandon a prosecution
- enfant délaissé = abandoned child; neglected child

délégation *f* delegation
- agir en vertu d'une délégation = to act on someone's authority
- agir par délégation = to act on someone's authority
- délégation de créance = assignment or delegation of debt
- délégation générale à la recherche scientifique = bureau for scientific research

27

déléguer *v* delegate (to); assign (to)

déliberé,-e *adj* deliberate; resolute; determined
- agir de propos déliberé = to act deliberately
- une affaire en délibéré = case under private consideration (by the judges)

délictuel,-elle *adj* delinquent; criminal

délictueux,-euse *adj* criminal
- fait délictueux = criminal act
- vagabondage délictueux = loitering with intent

délinquant *m*, **délinquante** *f*, (also *adj*) delinquent
- délinquant primaire = first offender
- mineurs délinquants = juvenile delinquents

délit *m* crime; (criminal) offence; offence; misdemeanour
- auteur d'un délit = tortfeasor
- délit civil = civil wrong; tort
- délit contre l'ordre public = breach of the peace
- délit d'initié = insider dealing or trading
- délit de fuite = failure to report an accident
- délit de presse = violation of laws governing the press
- délit grave = misdeed; serious offence
- délit pénal = offence (criminal)
- délit pénal mineur = non-indictable offence
- être pris en flagrant délit = to be caught red-handed, or in the act
- quasi-délit = quasi-delit; technical offence

délivrance *f* deliverance; rescue; release; issue; delivery
- délivrance d'un brevet = issue of a patent

délivrer *v* issue (to); serve (to)

demande *f* request; petition; application; claim
- à la demande de = at the instance of
- demande compensatoire = counter-claim
- demande en divorce = divorce petition
- demande en dommages-intérêts = claim for damages
- demande principale / accessoire / subsidiaire = main / secondary / contingency claim
- demande reconventionnelle = counter-claim

demander* *v* ask for (to); request (to); apply for (to); claim (to)

demandeur *m*, **demanderesse** *f* plaintiff; complainant; petitioner (in divorce)
- demandeur au civil = plaintiff
- demandeur au pourvoi = appellant
- demandeur d'un brevet = applicant for a patent
- demandeur en appel = appellant
- la partie demanderesse = the moving party

démarche *f* step; procedure
- démarche collective = joint representations
- démarches suspectes = suspicious proceedings
- les démarches nécessaires = the necessary steps

démence *f* dementia *(med)*; mental disorder; insanity; madness
- être en démence = to be of unsound mind; to be insane

démettre *v* dismiss (to)
- démettre quelqu'un de son appel = to dismiss someone's appeal

demeure *f* 1 residence; domicile; 2 delay
- à demeure = permanent; permanently
- en demeure = in arrears
- mettre quelqu'un en demeure de partir = to give someone notice to quit or leave
- meuble à demeure = fixture
- mise en demeure (de faire quelque chose) = formal notice or summons (to do something)
- sans plus longue demeure = without further delay

démission *f* resignation
- donner sa démission = to tender / hand in / give one's resignation

dénégation *f* denial; traverse
- dénégation d'écriture = denial / contestation of signature or writing
- dénégation de responsabilité = denial or disclaimer of responsibility

déni *m* denial
- déni de justice = miscarriage of justice

dénommer *v* denominate (to); designate

to); name (to)
- personne dénommée = nominee (for annuity)

dénonciation *f* official notice; notice of termination (eg of partnership); legal notice (of steps about to be taken); denunciation
- dénonciation calomnieuse = false accusation
- dénonciation de quelqu'un = information against someone

dépens (mpl) costs
- être condamné aux dépens = to be ordered to pay costs

déplacement *m* displacement; transfer; abduction
- déplacement d'enfant(s) = child abduction

déposant *m*, **déposante** *f* depositor (of money); bailor; deponent; witness

déposer* *v* 1 deposit (to); lay down (to); set down (to); 2 file (to); lodge (to); register (to); 3 give evidence (to); testify (to)
- déposer (en justice) contre = to give evidence against
- déposer son bilan = to go into (voluntary) liquidation; to file one's petition (in bankruptcy)
- déposer une marque de fabrique = to register a trade mark
- déposer une pétition = to file a petition
- déposer une plainte contre quelqu'un = to prefer a charge against someone; to lodge a complaint against someone

dépositaire *m,f* depository; trustee; bailee; agent
- dépositaire agréé = authorized dealer
- dépositaire de valeurs = holder of securities on trust
- dépositaire des enjeux = stake-holder
- dépositaire exclusif (de) = sole agent (for)
- dépositaire légal = escrow agent
- dépositaire public = authorized depository

déposition *f* evidence; (sworn) statement; deposition; testimony
- déposition rigoureuse en témoignage = affidavit
- recueillir une déposition = to take

someone's evidence
- signer sa déposition = to sign one's statement or deposition

dépôt *m* 1 deposit; depositing; lodgement; registration (trademark); bailment (of goods); 2 depository; depot; warehouse
- dépôt d'une marque de fabrique = registration of a trademark
- dépôt d'une pétition = filing of a petition
- dépôt de bilan = (volontary) liquidation
- dépôt de conclusions = to file submissions with court
- dépôt de garantie = deposit (as guarantee)
- dépôt du testament au rang des minutes du notaire = deposition of a will as a record with a notaire
- dépôt légal = registration of copyright
- dépôt préalable = advance deposit
- écroué au dépôt = committed to the cells
- en dépôt fiduciaire = in escrow
- il a passé la nuit au dépôt = he spent the night in the cells (in prison)
- mandat de dépôt = mittimus, committal, commitment (of prisoner)
- verser un dépôt = to pay a deposit

déprédation *f* depredation; damage; misappropriation; embezzlement

déroger *v* depart from (to)
- déroger à une condition = not to conform to a condition
- déroger de l'usage = to depart from custom
- déroger de la loi = to depart from the law

déroulement *m* progress; development (of events); unrolling; unwinding
- déroulement des travaux = progress of building work
- déroulement du contrat = progress of the contract

désaveu *m* retraction; disavowal; repudiation
- désaveu de paternité = repudiation of paternity; contestation of legitimacy

descendant,-e *adj*; **descendant** *m*, **descendante** *f* 1 descendent *adj*; 2 descendent
- descendant légitime = legitimate

29

descendent
- descendant naturel = natural descendent; illegitimate descendent
- ligne descendante = line of descent

déshérence *f* default of heirs; escheat
- succession en déshérence = intestate succession to which there are no next of kin
- tomber en déshérence = to escheat

désistement *m* withdrawal (of suit, defence, etc); waiver (of claim)

désister (se) *v* withdraw (to); stand down (to)
- se désister d'une demande = to waive a claim
- se désister d'une poursuite / action = to desist from an action

dessaisir *v* let go (to); release (to)
- dessaisir un tribunal d'une affaire = to remove a case from court
- être dessaisi du dossier = to be taken off the case
- le tribunal s'est dessaisi de l'affaire = the court decided not to proceed with the case
- se dessaisir *v* = to give up; to relinquish

dessaisissement *m* giving up; relinquishment; disseisin; dispossession

dessous-de-table *m* undercover payment; sum paid secretly to the vendor, in addition to the declared price, in a property deal; golden handshake

destination *f* 1 destination; 2 destination; intended purpose (of building, sum of money etc)
- destination du local = usage premises / dwelling will be put to (eg private or commercial)

détention *f* 1 holding (of securities, etc); possession (of fire arms, etc); 2 detention
- détention arbitraire = illegal imprisonment
- détention criminelle = imprisonment
- détention illégale des biens d'autrui = unlawful possession of other people's property
- détention préventive / provisoire = detention under remand
- maison de détention = remand home
- mettre en détention préventive = to remand in custody

détérioration *f* deterioration; damage (to property)
- détérioration volontaire = wilful damage

détournement *m* misappropriation; embezzlement
- détournement d'avion = hijacking of an aircraft
- détournement de biens = conversion of goods
- détournement de fonds = embezzlement
- détournement de mineur = abduction of a minor

devis *m* estimate; quotation; specification
- devis descriptif = detailed estimate; specification
- devis estimatif = preliminary estimate
- devis préliminaire = outline specification

devoir *m* duty
- devoir de confidentialité = duty of confidentiality
- impartir des devoirs à = to assign duties to
- manquement aux devoirs de la profession = unprofessional conduct

dévolution *f* devolution; transmission (of property, etc)

diffamation *f* slandering (verbal); libelling (written); defamation; slander; libel
- campagne de diffamation = smear campaign
- diffamation écrite = libel
- diffamation verbale = slander
- un procès en diffamation = an action for slander (verbal); an action for libel (written)

diffamatoire *adj* defamatory; slanderous; libellous

diffamer *v* slander (to); libel (to); defame (to)

différend *m* difference of opinion; disagreement; dispute
- différend entre deux parties = dispute between two parties
- différend relatis à ... = disagreement as to ...

différer *v* postpone (to)

diffuser *v* diffuse (to); spread (abroad) (to); circulate (to); broadcast (to)

dire *m* statement; assertion; allegation

- aux dires des ... = according to the statement of ...
- leurs dires ne concordent pas = their statements do not agree
- selon dire d'expert = according to expert opinion

dirigeant *m* manager

disciplinaire *adj* disciplinary
- les sanctions disciplinaires = disciplinary penalties
- procédure disciplinaire = disciplinary procedure

discrimination *f* discrimination
- discrimination raciale = racial discrimination

disparition *f* disappearance

disponibilité *f* availability
- disponibilité des biens = ability to transfer one's property; transferability of property

disponible *adj* available
- biens disponible = transferable property; disposable property
- le disponible = available assets or funds

disposer de *v* dispose (to); have (at one's disposal) (to)
- disposer d'un domaine par testament = to dispose of an estate in one's will
- la loi dispose que ... = the law provides that ...

dispositif *m* purview; enacting terms (of a statute, etc); pronouncement (judgement)

disposition* *f* disposition; arrangements *pl* disposal; provision; clause; stipulation
- arrêter des dispositions générales = to lay down general rules
- avoir la libre disposition de quelque chose = to be free to dispose of something
- dispositions à vue = drawings on an account
- disposition entre vifs = donation inter vivos
- disposition légale = statutory possibility
- dispositions testamentaires = provisions of a will; clauses of a will
- les dispositions contenues dans l'article 23 = the provisions of article 23
- sauf dispositions contraires = unless otherwise provided

dissimulation *f* dissimulation; dissembling; concealment
- dissimulation d'actif = concealment of assets

dissolution *f* dissolution (marriage, partnership, etc); disbanding; winding-up (eg of a company)

dissoudre *v* dissolve (to) (partnership, marriage, etc)

distorsion *f* distortion; imbalance; bias

distraction *f* absent-mindedness; abstraction
- distraction de fonds = misappropriation of funds

divertissement *m* 1 diversion; 2 misappropriation
- divertissement de fonds = misappropriation of funds

divorce *m* divorce
- cause de divorce = ground for divorce
- demande en divorce = petition for divorce
- demander le divorce = to file a petition for divorce; to sue for divorce
- divorce par consentement mutuel = divorce by mutual consent
- intenter une action en divorce (contre quelqu'un) = to take divorce proceedings (against someone)
- procédure de divorce = divorce proceedings

divorcer *v* divorce (to); get a divorce (to)
- divorcer d'avec sa femme / son mari = to divorce one's wife / husband
- se divorcer sa femme / son mari = to divorce one's wife / husband

divulgation *f* divulgence; disclosure

dol *m* fraud; fraudulent misrepresentation; dolus malus
- entaché de dol = tainted with fraud

dolosif,-ive *adj* fraudulent

domaine *m* estate; domain; property; demesne
- dans le domaine privé = in private ownership; in the private domain
- dans le domaine public = in the public domain
- domaine public, domaine de l'État = public property, State property
- invention tombée dans le domaine public

31

= invention for which the patent has expired
- ouvrage tombé dans le domaine public = work out of copyright

domicile *m* domicile; residence; registered address
- à domicile = at one's private address
- domicile légal = permanent residence; official domicile
- domicile principal = main residence
- quitter le domicile conjugal = to leave the marital home
- sans domicile; sans domicile fixe = of no fixed abode or address
- vente à domicile = door-to-door selling
- violation de domicile = illegal entry / forcible entry (of home)

dommage *m* damage; injury; loss; harm
- accorder / allouer des dommages et intérêts = to award damages
- causer un dommage = to cause damage; to make injury; to do mischief
- déclaration de dommages et intérêts = statement of claim
- dommage aux biens = damage to property
- dommage causé avec intention de nuire = malicious damage
- dommage réel = actual damage
- dommage subi = damage suffered; damage sustained
- dommage(s) corporel(s) = physical injury; personal injury
- dommage(s) matériel(s) = material damage
- dommages et intérêts / dommages-intérêts *mpl* = damages
- dommages et intérêts à titre exemplaire = exemplary damages
- dommages et intérêts à valeur répressive = punitive damages
- dommages et intérêts fixés au préalable = liqidated damages
- dommages et intérêts insignifiants = nominal damages
- dommages et intérêts non fixés au préalable = unliquidated damages
- dommages et intérêts pour préjudice moral = damages for pain and suffering
- dommages et intérêts réduits au strict minimum / franc symbolique = contemptuous damages
- dommages-intérêts accessoires = incidental damages
- dommages-intérêts moratoires = interest; arrears
- évaluer le dommage = to assess the damage
- montant des dommages et intérêts = award for damages
- poursuivre quelqu'un en dommages-intérêts = to sue someone for damages
- réparer un dommage = to make good a damage
- subir un dommage = to be harmed

dommageable *adj* detrimental; injurious; wrongful; tortious; prejudicial
- acte dommageable = tort

don *m* donation; gift
- don d'organes = donation of organs
- don manuel = personal gift (not requiring formal notarisation)
- recevoir quelque chose en don = to receive something as a gift

donataire *m,f* donee
donateur *m,* **donatrice** *f* donor
donation *f* donation; gift; settlement
- acte de donation entre vifs = deed of gift
- donation entre époux = donation between spouses
- donation entre vifs = donation inter vivos
- faire une donation à quelqu'un = to make a settlement on someone

dorénavant (adv) henceforth; hereafter
dormant,-e *adj* dormant; still; fixed; dead
- compte dormant = dead account (bank)

dossier *m* 1 dossier; documentation; 2 file; 3 case
- dossier d'une affaire = documents or file relating to a case
- dossier d'une procédure = brief
- dossier de permis de construire = application documents and plans required for the 'permis de construire'
- dossier médical = medical records
- dossier scolaire = school record
- établir le dossier d'une affaire = to brief

a case
- ouvrir / fermer un dossier = to open / close a case
- pièce qui incombe à un dossier = document which belongs to a dossier
- verser une pièce au dossier = to file a document

dot *f* dowry; marriage settlement in favour of daughter

dotation *f* endowment; emolument; grant

doter *v* provide with a dowry (to) (eg daughter); endow (to) (eg institution); give a grant to (to) (eg university)

double *m* duplicate; counterpart; double

dresser* *v* draw up (to)
- dresser plainte contre quelqu'un = to lodge a complaint against someone
- dresser une acte = to draw up an act
- dresser un procès-verbal = to report someone

drogue *f* drug
- drogue dur / douce = hard / soft drug

droit *m* (1) right; authority; claim; title
- à qui de droit = to whom it may concern
- avoir droit de regard sur = to have the right to examine or inspect
- avoir droit de regard dans la comptabilité = to be entitled to have access to the books and records
- de droit = of course, by right
- de droit comme de fait = both legitimately and effectively
- de droit et de fait = de facto and de jure
- droit à acquerir prioritairement = prior right of tenant to buy rented property when put up for sale
- droit au bail = right to the lease (of a property)
- droits civils = civil rights
- droits civiques = civic rights
- droit d'accession = right of accession / ownership
- droit d'aînesse = birthright
- droit d'asile = right of asylum
- droit de gage = lien
- droit de pacage = grazing rights
- droit de passage = right of way
- droit de préemption = pre-emptive right (right of precedence of one purchaser over another at the same purchase price)

- droit de préférence = right of first refusal
- droit de puisage = right to draw water
- droits de reproduction = reproduction rights (printed material)
- droit de suite = right of pursuit
- droit d'impression réservé = copyright
- droit d'usage = right of user
- droit de visite = (right of) access
- droit réel = title
- être en droit de faire = to have the right to do
- le droit de grève = the right to strike
- s'addresser à qui de droit = to apply to the proper quarter; to whom it may concern
- se réserver le droit de = to reserve the right to (eg publish, sell, distribute)

droit *m* (2) duty; duties; due; dues; fee
- droit d'accise = excise duty
- droit d'inscription = registration fee
- droit de mutation (entre vifs) = transfer duty, conveyance duty
- droit de mutation (par décès) = succession duty
- droit de timbre = stamp duty
- droit de recommandation = registration fee (post)
- droits d'auteur = royalties
- droits d'enregistrement = property transfer registration costs
- droits de succession = duties on estate (of deceased person); estate duties; death duties; inheritance tax
- droits de succession (par testament) = probate duty; inheritance tax
- exempt de droits = duty-free
- passible de droits = liable to duty

droit *m* (3) law
- droit administratif = administrative law
- droit basé sur le droit jurisprudentiel = common law
- droit civil = civil law
- droit commercial = commercial law
- droit communautaire = EC law
- droit coutumier, droit commun = common law
- droit de contrats = contract law
- droit de la consommation = consumer law

- droit de la famille = family law
- droit de la responsabilité = law of tort
- droit de contrats = contract law
- droit des obligations = law of contract
- droit des sociétés = company law
- droit écrit = written law, statute law
- droit fiscal = Revenue law; taxation law
- droit français = French law
- droit national = municipal law
- droit pénal, droit criminel = criminal law
- droit privé = private law or right
- droit procédural = adjective law; procedural law
- droit public = public law or right
- faire le droit = to study law
- fond du droit = substantive law
- par voies de droit = by legal process
- point de droit = point of law
- question de droit = issue / question of law

dû, due *adj* due; owing
- contrat rédigé en bonne et due forme = contract drawn up in due form; formal contract
- dû à = due to
- en temps dû = in due course

dudit, desdit(e)s (see ledit) of the aforesaid; of the aforementioned

duplicata *m,inv* duplicate

durée *f* length; duration

E

échapper *v* escape (to); be beyond (to)
- cela échappe à notre juridiction = it is outside our jurisdiction
- échapper à l'impôt = to avoid paying income tax
- échapper aux recherches = to escape detection
- faire échapper un prisonnier = to help a prisoner escape

échéance *f* date of payment; date of maturity; due date; expiry; settlement date; expiration of tenancy
- demander une prolongation d'échéance = to ask for an extension of time
- échéance du bail = expiration of lease
- échéance fatale = death; *(fig)* the day of reckoning
- l'échéance d'une police = expiration of a policy
- payable à l'échéance = payable when due; payable at maturity
- venir à échéance = to fall due

échéant *adj* falling due; payable
- le cas échéant = should the occasion / case arises; if need be; if necessary

échoir *v* fall due (to) (eg rent); be payable (to)
- échoir à quelqu'un = to fall to someone's share
- intérêts échus = outstanding interest; due interest *(fin)*
- payer son loyer à terme échu = to pay one's rent in arrears

éclaircissement *m* clarification; clearing up; explanation
- demande d'éclaircissement = request for clarification

écouter *v* hear (to); listen to (to)
- écoute téléphonique = telephone tapping

écrit *m* document; written document; piece of writing; written exam or paper
- consigner / coucher quelque chose par écrit = to set down something in writing
- convention en écrit; convention par écrit = agreement in writing
- exposer un cas par écrit = to submit a written statement of a case
- par écrit = in writing

effet *m* effect; result
- effet dévolutif = process of devolving case onto Court of Appeal
- effet obligatoire = binding effect
- effet pervers = opposite effect
- effet relatif = relative effect; privity
- effet suspensif = suspensive effect
- effets personnels = personal effects
- être / rester sans effet = to be ineffective; to have no effect
- prendre effet à la date de = to take effect from; to be operative from

effraction *f* breaking and entering; breaking-in
- à l'épreuve de l'effraction =

burglar-proof
- effraction informatique = computer hacking
- entrer par effraction = to break in

égalité *f* equality
- clause d'égalité = equality clause
- égalité de rémunération = equal pay
- égalité des droits = equal rights
- égalité des salaires = equal pay

élargir *v* 1 widen (to); broaden (to); enlarge (to); 2 release (to); free (to) (prisoner)

élevé,-e *adj* high; heavy; substantial
- dommages-intérêts élevés = substantial damages

émancipation *f* emancipation; liberation

émanciper *v* emancipate (to); liberate (to)

embaucher *v* engage (to) (staff etc); take on (to); sign on (to) (workmen etc)
- réembauchage = re-engagement (of staff)

émeute *f* riot; disturbance
- excite une émeute = to stir up a riot

émoluments *mpl* emoluments

empêchement *m* obstacle (unexpected); hitch; impediment
- empêchement de la langue = impediment of speech

emploi *m* job; post; employment
- perte d'emploi = loss of job; loss of employment
- privation partielle d'emploi = partial loss of employment; part time working

employé *m*, **employée** *f* employee

employeur *m* employer
- responsabilité de l'employeur = employer's liability

empoisonnement *m* poisoning

empreinte *f* impression; imprint; footprint; fingerprint
- empreintes digitales = fingerprints
- empreinte génétique = genetic fingerprint

emprisonnement *m* imprisonment
- emprisonnement à vie = life imprisonment
- emprisonnement cellulaire = solitary confinement

emprunt *m* loan; borrowing
- contracter un emprunt = to raise a loan
- emprunt-logement *m* = house purchase loan; mortgage
- route d'emprunt = alternative road; by-pass

enfant *m* child; infant
- abandon d'enfant = abandonment of a child
- déclarer un enfant à la mairie = to register a (new-born) child at the town hall
- déplacement d'enfant(s) = child abduction
- enfant adultérin = child related to one of a married couple but born of an adulterous relationship
- enfant délaissé = abandoned child; neglected child
- enfant en tutelle = child under guardianship
- enfant incestueux = child born of incest
- enfant légitime / illégitime = legitimate / illegitimate child
- enfant mineur = minor
- enfant naturel = natural child; illegitimate child
- enfant problème; enfant difficile = problem child; difficult child
- intérêt de l'enfant = child welfare
- mourir sans enfants = to die without issue
- protection de l'enfant = child care
- reconnaissance d'un enfant naturel = recognition of an illegitimate child
- sévices exercés sur un enfant = child abuse

engagement *m* engagement; obligation; promise; commitment; agreement; contract; liability; mortgaging (of estate)
- engagement signé par la caution = bail-bond
- faire face à ses engagements = to meet one's liabilities
- signer un engagement = to sign an agreement

engager* *v* bind (to); commit (to); undertake (to) institute (to) (proceedings, action)
- engager par contrat = to contract
- engager une action judiciaire = to take legal action

enlèvement *m* abduction; removal

- enlèvement d'enfant = baby snatching
- enlèvement de mineur = abduction

énoncé *m* statement; declaration; exposition; expression of; terms; wording
- énoncé d'un acte = wording of an act

énoncer *v* express (to); state (to)

enquête *f* inquiry; inquest (on a dead person); investigation (eg by police); survey
- conseil / commission d'enquête = court of enquiry
- enquête judiciaire après mort d'homme = (coroner's) inquest
- faire une enquête = to make an investigation
- mener / conduire une enquête = to lead / be in charge of an investigation
- ouvrir une enquête = to set up or open an inquiry

enquêter *v* hold an inquiry (to); investigate (to); conduct a survey (to)
- enquêter sur une affaire = to inquire into an affair

enregistrement *m* recording; registration; registry
- droits / frais d'enregistrement = registration fees; stamp duty
- enregistrement d'une société = registration of a company
- enregistrement du testament = registration of a will for public record

enregistrer *v* record (to); register (to); enter (to); note (to)
- enregistrer les affaires = to list the cases, lawsuits
- enregistrer un acte = to register a deed
- enregistrer une naissance = to register a birth
- une société enregistrée = an incorporated company

enseignement *m* education

entacher *v* 1 sully (to); taint (to); blemish (to); 2 vitiate (to)
- acte entaché d'un vice radical = act vitiated by a fundamental flaw
- entaché de dol = tainted with fraud
- entaché de nullité = null and void
- transaction entaché de fraude = fraudulent transaction

entendre *v* hear (to); listen to (to)

- entendre les témoins = to hear the witnesses

entente *f* understanding; agreement
- entente entre enchérisseurs = knock-out agreement
- entente délictueuse = conspiracy
- ententes illicites = illegal agreements

entraide *f (no pl)* mutual aid
- entraide judiciaire internationale = international judicial cooperation

entraîner* *v* attract (to); carry (to)
- entraîner une condamnation au pénal = to attract a sentence under criminal law

entrave *f* hindrance; restriction (eg of liberty)
- circulation sans entrave = free-flowing traffic
- entraves à la saisine de la justice = hindrance of submission to justice

entrepreneur *m*, **entrepreneuse** *f* builder; contractor

entreprise *f* business; firm
- contrat d'entreprise = business contract; company contract
- placer une entreprise entre les mains d'un liquidateur = to put a company into receivership

envoi *m* sending; delivery (of goods); consignment
- envoi de fonds = remittance of cash
- envoi en possession = livery of seisin; writ of possession

épave *f* wreck; stray; derelict (lost object); unclaimed object; ownerless (animal); write-off (damaged car)

époux *m*, **épouse** *f* spouse; husband, wife
- époux survivant = surviving spouse

épreuve *f* proof; test; ordeal
- mettre à l'épreuve = to put on probation
- mise à l'épreuve = probation

équipments *mpl* fixtures and fittings

erreur *f* mistake; error
- erreur de bonne foi = genuine error
- erreur de droit = mistake of law
- erreur de fait = mistake of fact
- erreur judiciaire = miscarriage of justice
- faire erreur = to be mistaken
- induire délibérément en erreur = to give a false impression

escroquer *v* swindle (to); defraud (to)
escroquerie *f* swindle; swindling; fraud
- escroquerie au chantage = blackmail racket
- être victime d'une escroquerie = to be a victim of fraud
- tentative d'escroquerie = attempted fraud
espionnage *m* espionage; spying
- espionnage industriel = industrial espionage
essai *m* test; trial
- période d'essai = probationary period; trial period
ester *v* appear (to); stand (to)
- ester en jugement = to appear in court; to plead
- ester en justice = to go to court; to appear in court (as plaintiff or defendant); to sue
établir *v* establish (to); set up (to) (eg agency); put up (to) (eg building); draw up (to) (eg plan); write (to) (eg cheque); fix (to) (eg price) lay out (to) (eg conditions)
- établir une accusation = to make out a case; to substantiate a charge
- établir un chèque à l'ordre de = to write a cheque to
établissement* *m* establishment; establishing
- établissement commercial = commercial establishment
- établissement public autonome = government-owned corporation
- établissement stable = fixed place of business
état *m* 1 state; condition; 2 statement; list; return; account
- à l'état de projet = at the planning stage
- actes de l'état civil = certificates of births, marriages, deaths
- affaire en état = suit ready for hearing
- en bon état = in good repair (eg house)
- en état = in order
- en état de marche = in working order
- état civil = civil status, marital status
- état de frais = statement of expenses
- état des lieux = report of state of accomodation; inventory of fixtures
- état pro forma = pro forma statement

- remettre en état = to refurbish / renovate; to recondition
éteindre *v* extinguish (to); put out (to); turn off (to); switch off (to)
- éteindre une dette = to extinguish a debt
étranger,-ère *adj*, **étranger** *m*, **étrangère** *f* 1 foreign; strange; 2 foreigner; stranger
évasion *f* escape
éviction *f* eviction; dispossession
évincer *v* evict (to); oust (to)
exception *f* exception; incidental plea (of defence)
- exception d'inexécution = plea for non-performance
- exception de procédure = proceedings on incidental plea of defence; procedural plea
- exception péremptoire = demurrer, plea in bar
- juridiction d'exception = jurisdiction of an exceptional court
- opposer une exception = to demur; to raise an objection in law
- première exception = plea (defendant's)
- tribunal d'exception = emergency court; special court
excès *m* excess; surplus
- excès de pouvoir = action ultra vires; abuse of power
- excès de vitesse = breaking / exceeding the speed limit
excitation *f* excitation; stimulation; incitement
- excitation à = incitement to
exclusif,-ive *adj* exclusive
- dépositaire exclusif (de) = sole agent (for)
- mandat exclusif = exclusive selling order (single agent)
exclusion *f* exclusion; expulsion; suspension
- à l'exclusion de = with the exception of
exécuter *v* execute (to); carry out (to); perform (to) (eg contract); enforce (to) (eg law, writ, etc)
- faire exécuter un jugement = to enforce a judgement
exécuteur *m*, **exécutrice** *f* executor, executrix; enforcer; executioner

37

- exécuteur / exécutrice testamentaire = executor / executrix (of a will)

exécution *f* execution; carrying out; implementation; enforcement (eg of law); distraint; distress
- en exécution de la loi = in compliance with the law; in accordance with the law
- exécution d'un jugement = enforcement of a judgement
- exécution en nature = specific performance
- exécution forcée = execution of a writ; enforcement
- exécution provisoire = provisional enforcement (of a judgement)

exécutoire *adj & m* 1 executory; enforceable (of decree, contract, etc); 2 writ of execution
- délivrer un exécutoire pour le montant des dépens = to issue an execution for the amount of the costs
- exécutoire de dépens = order to pay costs
- jugement exécutoire = final judgement
- mesure exécutoire pour chaque partie contractante = measure which is binding on each contracting party
- obligation exécutoire = operative obligation

exemplaire *m* copy; exemplar

exemption *f* exemption

exéquatur *m* enforcement of a judicial decision

exercer *v* exercise (to); exert (to); practise (to)
- exercer des poursuites contre quelqu'un = to bring an action against someone
- exercer ses droits = to exercise one's rights
- exercer un mandate = to carry out a mandate
- exercer un métier = to follow a trade / profession

exhumation *f* exhumation
- permis d'exhumer = exhumation order

expédition *f* copy or certified copy (of deed, contract etc); disposal (of a business, etc); dispatch (of parcel, etc); consignment
- bulletin d'expédition = waybill

- en double / triple expédition = in duplicate / triplicate
- expédition en douane = customs clearance

expert *v* expert
- expert agréé = independent expert
- expert-comptable = chartered accountant
- expert judiciaire = expert witness

expertise *f* expert valuation / appraisal; survey; surveyor's report
- expertise d'un bien = valuation of a property

expiration *f* expiration
- expiration d'un terme = effluxion of time
- expiration du bail = expiration of lease
- l'expiration des délais = time limit

explicite *adj* express; clear

exploit *m* 1 exploit; achievement; 2 writ; process; summons; notice
- dresser un exploit = to draw up a writ
- exploit d'huissier = writ
- signifier un exploit à quelqu'un = to serve a writ on someone

explosif *m* explosive

exposé *m* statement; account; exposition; preamble
- donner un exposé d'un projet = to sketch out a plan
- faire un exposé = to read a paper; to give an account

exprès,-esse *adj* express; distinct; explicit
- par exprès = express delivery

expressément *adv* expressly; explicitly

expropriation *f* compulsory purchase of private property; expropriation; compulsory surrender of real estate

exproprier *v* put a compulsory purchase order (to) (eg on house, land)
- exproprier quelqu'un = to put a compulsory purchase order on someone's property

extinction *f* extinction; extinguishment
- extinction d'un contrat = termination of a contract
- extinction d'un hypothèque = extinction of a mortgage; paying off of a mortgage
- extinction d'une dette = paying off of a debt

extorsion *f* extortion

F

façon *f* manner; mode
- assigner quelqu'un en contre façon = to bring an action for infringement of patent against someone
- en aucune façon = in no event

faculté *f* faculty; right; option; power; freedom
- avoir la faculté de faire quelque chose = to have the option of doing something

faillite *f* bankruptcy; insolvency; failure
- déclarer quelqu'un en faillite = to declare someone bankrupt
- liquidateur de faillite ; liquidateur judiciaire = official liquidator / receiver
- syndic de faillite = assignee; official receiver; public trustee (in bankruptcy)

fait* *m* fact; event; occurrence
- aller droit au fait = to go straight to the point
- de fait = de facto
- en fait et en droit = in fact and in law
- fait accompli = fait accompli; accomplished fact
- fait délictueux = criminal act
- faits constatés = known facts
- faits litigieux = contentious facts
- il me faut des faits concrets = I must have some concrete facts
- les faits qui lui sont reprochés = the charges against him
- reconnaissez-vous les faits? = do you accept the facts?

faute *f* error; mistake; negligence; offence; fault
- commettre une faute = to commit a misdemeanour or offence
- faute civile = civil wrong
- faute de conduite = driving error; driving offence
- faute de la victime = contributory negligence
- faute de service = act of (administrative) negligence
- faute grave = gross negligence
- faute lourde = gross misconduct (employee)
- faute pénale = criminal offence
- faute professionnelle = professional misconduct

faux *m* falsehood; fake; forgery
- faire un faux = to commit a forgery
- inscription de faux = procedure in proof that document has been forged
- pour faux et usage de faux = for forgery and using forgeries

faux, fausse *adj* false; untrue; fake; forged
- acte faux = forged deed
- fausse alerte = false alarm
- fausse monnaie = counterfeit coinage or currency
- faux nom = false or assumed name
- faux témoignage = perjury

femme *f* woman; wife
- femme au foyer = housewife
- femme battue = battered wife
- femme d'action = working woman
- femme d'affaires = businesswoman
- femme d'intérieur = homemaker; housewife
- femme de charge = housekeeper
- femme de ménage = domestic help; cleaning lady
- femme de service = cleaner; dinner lady
- femme enceinte = pregnant woman; expectant mother
- femme mariée = married woman
- femme médecin = lady doctor
- femme professeur = lady teacher
- la femme Colpin = the woman, the accused, Colpin

fermage *m* 1 farm rent; rent paid for use of arable land; 2 tenant farming

ferme *f* 1 farm; farmhouse; 2 farm lease
- petite ferme = smallholding
- prendre une terre à ferme = to farm land (on lease)

Fichier Central des dispositions de dernières volontés (France) Central Register for the filing of wills
- Registre Central des dispositions de dernière volonté (Belgique) = Central Register for the filing of wills
- Registre Central des Testaments = Central Register for the filing of wills

fidéicommis *m* trust; trusteeship
- acte de fidéicommis = trust deed

fidéicommissaire *m* trustee; beneficiary of a trust

fidéicommissariat *m* trusteeship

fidéicommisser *v* make a trust (to); leave a trust (to)

fiduciaire *adj & m* 1 fiduciary; 2 trustee; fiduciary
- certificat fiduciaire = trustee's certificate
- en dépôt fiduciaire = in escrow
- héritier fiduciaire = heir; trustee
- société fiduciaire = trust company

fiduciairement *adv* fiduciarily; in trust

fief *m* fief

filiation *f* filiation; consanguinity in direct line; descendents
- en filiation directe = in direct line
- filiation adoptive = affiliation by adoption
- filiation légitime = legitimate filiation; legitimate lineage
- filiation naturelle = natural filiation

filouterie *f* swindle; fraud; stealing; swindling

fin *f* end; close
- aux fins de la présente loi = for the purposes of this act
- chômeur en fin de droits = unemployed person no longer entitled to receive (state) benefit
- fin d'exercice = end of financial year
- fin de non-recevoir = demurrer; objection
- rendre une fin de non-recevoir = to dismiss a case
- renvoyé des fins de la plainte = discharged, acquitted
- renvoyer quelqu'un des fins de sa plainte = to nonsuit someone

fiscalité *f* tax system; taxation system; fiscality
- le poids de la fiscalité = the tax burden; the tax load

foi *f* faith; (pledged) word
- en foi de quoi j'ai décidé = in witness whereof I have decided; on the strength of which I have decided
- les deux textes feront foi = both texts shall be considered authentic
- sous la foi de serment = under oath; on oath
- sur la foi des témoins = on the word / testimony of witnesses

folie *f* madness; folly

fonctionnaire *m,f* official; civil servant
- fonctionnaire de police = police officer

fond* *m* bottom; heart; content; substance
- défense sans fond = peremptory defence
- fond d'un procès = main issue of a suit
- le fond de l'affaire = the substance of the case
- le fond du problème = the heart or root of the problem
- le fond et la forme = content and form

fondateur *m*, **fondatrice** *f* founder; promoter; incorporator (company)
- membre fondateur / fondatrice = founder member
- parts de fondateur / fondatrice = founder's shares

fondé,-e *adj*; **fondé** *m* de pouvoir 1 well-founded; justified; 2 authorized representative
- bien fondé = well-founded
- fondé de procuration spéciale et authentique = attorney
- fondé sur des ouï-dire = based on hearsay
- il est le fondé de pouvoir de ... = he holds a power of attorney for ...
- mal fondé = ill-founded; groundless

fondement *m* foundation
- fondement d'une action en justice = cause of action
- sans fondement = without foundation; groundless

fonds *m* 1 land; estate; 2 funds
- cultiver un fonds = to cultivate a piece of land
- fonds de terre = piece of land or estate; tenement; hereditament

force *f* force; strength
- avoir force exécutoire = enforceable
- force majeure = circumstances beyond one's control
- force publique = the police

forclore *v* foreclose (to) (a mortgage); debar (to); bar (to); estop (to)
- forclos = time barred
- se laisser forclore = to fail to make a

claim within the statutory time-limit
forclusion *f* foreclosure; debarment; barring
forfait *m* fixed rate; fixed price; contract;
fixed-sum contract
- forfait fixe = fixed sum
- forfait journalier = individual contribution
  towards cost of state hospital care
- gain forfait = capital gain
- prix à forfait = lump sum
forfaitairement *adv* inclusively; on an
inclusive basis
forfaiture *f* abuse of authority;
maladministration; malfeasance
formalité *f* formality; formal procedure
- remplir une formalité = to comply with a
  formality
formation *f* formation; training; panel
- en formation plénière = in a full court
- formation professionnelle = vocational
  training; further education
- formation restreinte = bench of three
  judges (instead of five) in the Cour de
  Cassation
- plan de formation = training scheme
forme *f* form; shape
- arrêt cassé pour vice de forme =
  judgement quashed on a technical point
  or a point of law
- avertir quelqu'un dans les formes = to
  give someone formal warning
- faire une réclamation en forme = to
  make or put in a formal request
- formes juridiques = legal formalities
frais *m,mpl* fees; cost; expenses;
expenditure
- frais à la charge de ... = costs payable
  by ...
- frais accidentels = incidental expenses
- frais d'enregistrement = registration fees
- frais d'entretien = maintenance costs
  (eg of estate)
- frais de dossier = mortgage arrangement
  fee
- frais de gestion = administration
  expenses
- frais de justice = legal costs; court costs
- frais divers = sundry charges
- frais en sus = additional charges / costs
- frais judiciaires = legal charges
franc, franche *adj* 1 free; 2 frank;

straightforward; 3 clear
- accord franc et massif = unequivocal
  acceptance
- franc d'impôts = exempt from taxation
- trois jours francs = three clear days
fraude *f* fraud; deception
- fraude civile = fraud; wilful
  misrepresentation
- fraude fiscale = tax evasion
- fraude pénale = cheating
frustrer *v* frustrate (to); defraud (to)
- frustrer quelqu'un de quelque chose = to
  defraud someone of something

G

gage *m* security; pledge; pledged or
pawned article
- droit de gage = lien
- mettre en gage = to pawn
gagnant,-e *adj* winning
- la partie gagnante = the prevailing party
gain *m* earnings; wages; gain; winning
- donner gain de cause à quelqu'un = to
  decide the case in favour of someone
- gain de la femme mariée = wife's earned
  income
- gain forfait = capital gain
garant *m*, **garante** *f* guarantor; surety;
guarantee
- garant d'une dette = surety for a debt
- prendre quelqu'un à garant quelque
  chose = to call someone to witness
  something
- servir de garant à quelqu'un = to act as
  guarantor for someone
garantie *f* guarantee; security; collateral;
warranty
- dépôt de garantie = deposit (as
  guarantee)
- fonds déposés ou détenus en garantie =
  funds lodged or held as security
- garantie bancaire = bank guarantee
- garantie extrinsèque = guarantee
  supported by financial institution
- garantie intrinsèque = guarantee

unsupported by financial institution
- garanties fondamentales = fundamental safeguards
- les garanties individuelles = laws for the protection of individuals
- sous garantie = under warranty

garantir *v* guarantee (to); warrant (to)
- garantir quelqu'un contre = to indemnify someone from / against
- garantir une dette = to guarantee a debt

garde *f* guardianship; care; custody (eg of children after divorce)
- accorder le droit de garde = to grant custody
- c'est la mère qui a eu la garde de l'enfant = the mother was given custody of the child
- droit de garde = custody; custodianship
- droit de garde effectif = actual custody (of a child)
- droit de garde juridique = legal custody (of a child)
- être placé en garde à vue = to be kept in police custody; to be held for questioning
- garde d'enfants = child minder; child minding
- Garde des sceaux = Minister of Justice
- garde juridique = legal liability

garder *v* keep (to); guard (to); look after (to)
- garder quelqu'un à vue = to keep someone in custody; to keep a close watch on someone

gestion *f* management; handling
- frais de gestion = administration expenses
- gestion administrative = administration
- gestion de patrimoine = estate management; private assets management
- gestion tutelaire = guardianship

grâce *f* grace; clemency; free pardon
- demander grâce pour quelqu'un = to appeal for clemency for someone
- lettre(s) de grâce = reprieve

graffiti *mpl* graffiti

gratification *f* gratuity; bonus

greffe *m* registrar (of commercial court)

greffier *m*, **greffière** *f* clerk of the court

- greffier en chef = chief clerk

grève *f* strike
- être en grève = to be on strike
- grève de solidarité = sympathetic strike
- grève du zèle = work-to-rule strike
- grève perlée = go-slow strike
- se mettre en grève = to go on strike

grever *v* entail (to) (an estate); mortgage (to) (property); burden (to); encumber (to); impose a rate on (to) (building)
- héritage grevé de dettes = encumbered estate / inheritance
- le bâtiment est grevé d'hypothèques = the building is mortgaged to the hilt

gréviste *m,f* striker

grivèlerie *f* offence of ordering a meal, etc in a restaurant without being able to pay for it

grossesse *f* pregnancy
- interruption volontaire de grossesse (IVG) = termination of pregnancy

H

habile *adj* clever; skilful; fit; competent
- habile à succéder = able, competent to inherit

habilitation *f* capacitation; authorization
- habilitation de quelqu'un à faire quelque chose = enabling of someone to do something

habilité *f* ability; competency; title
- avoir habilité à hériter = to be entitled to inherit

habiliter *v* capacitate (to); authorize (to); enable (to); empower (to)
- être habilité à faire quelque chose = to be enabled to do something
- représentant dûment habilité = duly authorized officer

habitation *f* house; dwelling
- immeuble d'habitation = block of flats
- local d'habitation = dwelling; residential unit; domestic premises
- police multirisques habitation = building insurance policy

- taxe d'habitation = community charge; rates

handicapé *m*, **handicapée** *f* disabled person

harcèlement *m* harassment
- harcèlement sexuel = sexual harassment

hérédité *f* heredity; right of inheritance
- expilation d'hérédité = depredation of decedent's estate

héritage *m* inheritance; heritage
- faire un héritage = to receive a legacy

hériter *v* inherit (to); succeed (to)
- hériter de quelqu'un = to inherit someone's estate

héritier *m*, **héritière** *f* heir; heiress; next-of-kin; legatee
- héritier présomptif = next-of-kin; heir apparent
- héritier réservataire = heir who cannot be completely disinherited
- héritier testamentaire = legatee

heure *f* hour; time
- faire des heures supplémentaires = to do or work overtime
- les heures supplémentaires = extra hours; overtime hours

hoirie *f* inheritance; succession
- avancement d'hoirie = advancement; settlement of portion by anticipation

homicide *adj & m,f* 1 homicidal; 2 murderer, murderess; 3 murder; homicide
- homicide accidentel = death by misadventure
- homicide de soi-même = suicide; felo de se
- homicide excusable = justifiable homicide
- homicide involuntaire = manslaughter
- homicide par imprudence = manslaughter
- homicide volontaire = murder; voluntary manslaughter

homicidé,-e *adj* murdered
- personne homicidée = murdered person

homologation *f* official approval; homologation; probate (of will)

homologuer *v* approve (to); confirm (to); endorse (to); sanction (to)
- homologuer un testament = to prove a will

honoraires *mpl* fee(s); honorarium; retainer

(lawyer's); royalty (author's)
- les honoraires de l'architecte = architect's fee

huis *m* **clos** closed hearing; hearing in camera
- entendre une cause à huis clos = to hear a case in camera
- ordonner un huis clos = to order proceedings to be held in camera
- rendre un jugement à huis ouvert = to pronounce jugement in open court

huissier *m* bailiff; process server; court usher; court porter
- huissier-audencier = court usher
- huissier de justice = bailiff

huitaine *f* about eight days; about a week; a week
- sous huitane = within a week
- un cas remis à huitane = case adjourned for a week

hypothèque *f* mortgage
- hypothéquer *v* = to mortgage; to secure by mortgage
- lever/prendre une hypothèque = to raise a mortgage
- purge d'hypothèque = redemption of mortgage

hypothétique *adj* hypothetical

I

icelui, icelle, iceux, icelles *pron* (= **celui-ci, celle-ci, ceux-ci, celles-ci**) the one, those *pl*, he, she

idoine *adj* appropriate; fitting; fit; able
- apte et idoine à tester = fit and competent to make a will

illégal *adj* unlawful; illegal

illicite *adj* wrongful; illicit
- ententes illicites = illegal agreements

immeuble *adj & m* 1 real; immovable; 2 building; block of flats; (business) premises; real estate; real property
- biens immeubles = real estate or property
- immeuble à usage locatif = block of

rented flats
- immeuble d'habitation = block of flats; residential building
- immeuble de bureaux = office block
- immeuble mixte = house or building situated in a mixed residential and commercial area

immixtion *f* 1 unwarranted interference (in an affair); 2 assumption
- immixtion dans une succession = assumption of a succession

immobilier,-ière *adj* property; estate
- agent immobilier = estate agent
- biens immobiliers = real estate

immobilisation *f* immobilization; conversion into an immovable (property)
- immobilisations = fixed assets; capital assets

immobiliser *v* immobilize (to); convert into immovables (to) (property); tie up (to) (capital)

immunité *f* immunity
- immunité diplomatique = diplomatic immunity

impartir *v* grant (to) (eg right); assign (to) (eg a duty)
- délai imparti = time limit
- impartir des devoirs à = to assign duties to
- impartir des pouvoirs à = to invest powers in
- impartir un délai à = to grant an extension to

impératif,-ve *adj* urgent; imperative; mandatory

impétrant *m*, **impétrante** *f* applicant; grantee (eg of diploma)

impôt *m* tax; tax liability; taxation; tax rate; levy
- déclaration d'impôt = tax return
- dégrèvement d'impôt = tax allowance; tax cut
- impôt additionnel = surtax
- impôt foncier = land tax; property tax
- impôt retenu à la source = witholding tax
- impôt sur le revenu = income tax
- impôt sur les plus-values = capital gains tax
- impôts cédulaires = scheduled taxes

(income tax)
- receveur des impôts = tax collector

imprévision *f* lack of foresight; improvidence

imprescriptibilité *f* imprescriptibility; indefeasibility (eg of a right)

imprescriptible *adj* imprescriptible; indefeasible

imprudence *f* carelessness; imprudence
- blessures par imprudence = injuries through negligence
- homicide par imprudence = manslaughter through negligence

impubère *adj & m,f* below the age of puberty; minor

imputabilité *f* imputability

inabrogeable *adj* unrepealable

inadmissibilité *f* inadmissibility

inadmissible *adj* inadmissible

inaliénabilité *f* inalienability; indefeasibility

inamovibilité *f* permanence; irremovability; fixity of tenure

inamovible *adj* irremovable; fixed
- agencements inamovibles d'un bâtiment = fixtures of a building

inaptitude *f* inaptitude; unfitness; unsuitability

incapable *adj & m,f* 1 incapable *adj*; incompetent *adj*; 2 incapable person; incapacitated person
- incapable de tester = not competent to make a will
- les (majeures) incapables = the legally incapacitated

incapacité *f* incompetence; incapability; disability; legal incapacity
- en état d'incapacité légale = dclared incapable of managing one's affairs
- frapper quelqu'un d'incapacité = to incapacitate or disqualify someone
- incapacité civile / juridique = civil / legal incapacity
- incapacité d'exercice = incapacity to exercise a right
- incapacité de jouissance = incapacity to enjoy a right
- incapacité totale de travail = total incapacity to work

incarcération *f* imprisonment; incarceration

incendie *m* fire outbreak; arson

- incendie criminel = arson
inceste *m* incest
incestueux,-euse *adj & m,f* 1 incestuous;
2 person guilty of incest
- enfant incestueux = child born of incest
incident,-e *adj,* incident *m* 1 incidental;
2 incident; point of law
- multiplier les incidents = to bring
forward innumerable points
incitation *f* incitement; inciting
- incitation à la haine raciale = incitement
to racial hatred
incompétent,-e *adj* incompetent; not
qualified (to try case)
incompatibilité *f* incompatibility
- incompatibilité d'humeur =
temperamental incompatibility
incompétence *f* incompetence; lack of
authority; lack of jurisdiction
- incompétence territoriale =
incompetency ratione loci
inculpation *f* charge; indictment
- inculpation de vol = on a charge of theft
inculpé *m,* **inculpée** *f* (l') the accused
- inculpé de complicité = charged with
complicity
indemniser *v* indemnify (to); compensate
(to)
- indemniser quelqu'un d'une perte = to
compensate someone for a loss
- se faire indemniser = to receive
compensation
indemnité *f* indemnity; compensation (for
loss sustained); benefit; allowance
- demander une indemnité (en
dommages-intérêts) = to put in a claim
for damages / compensation
- indemnité de chômage = unemployment
benefit
- indemnité de clientèle = payment for
goodwill (business purchase)
- indemnité de licenciement = dismissal
payment; severance pay
- indemnité de logement = housing
allowance
- indemnité de vie chère = cost-of-living
allowance
- indemnité journalière = sick pay
- indemnité pour accidents de travail =
industrial injuries benefit

- indemnité pour surestaries = demurrage
indice *m* indication; sign; clue; piece of
evidence; index; rating
indigne *adj* undeserving; disqualified
- indigne de succéder = disqualified /
debarred from inheriting
indirect,-e *adj* indirect (eg tax, line of
descent); circumstantial (evidence)
indisponible *adj* not available; unavailable;
inalienable (property); entailed (estate)
individualisation *f* individualization; tailoring
to individual requirements
- individualisation d'une peine =
sentencing according to characteristics
of the offender; individualization of
sentencing
individualiser *v* individualize (to)
indivis,-e *adj* undivided; joint (eg owner,
estate)
- posséder par indivis = to possess jointly
- propriétaire indivis = joint owner
indivisaire *m,f* joint owner; tenant in
common
indivisément *adv* jointly
- posséder une ferme indivisément = to
have joint ownnership of a farm
indivisibilité *f* indivisibility
indivision *f* joint possession; joint
ownership
- propriété en indivision = jointly held
property
indu *adj* 1 not owed, not due (money);
2 against the regulations
- paiement de l'indu = payment of money
not owed
- répétition d'indu = recovery of payment
made by mistake
indulgence *f* leniency
indulgent *adj* lenient
inefficacité *f* ineffectiveness; inefficacy
- inefficacité du testament = ineffectiveness of a will (eg due to later will)
inexécution *f* non-performance; breach of
contract
infamant,-e *adj* 1 defamatory; 2 ignominious; dishonourable
- peine infamant = penalty involving loss
of civil rights
infirmatif,-ive *adj* invalidating; nullifying;
quashing

45

infirmation *f* invalidation; annulment; quashing
infirmer *v* invalidate (to); annul (to); quash (to)
information *f* 1 inquiry; 2 information; piece of information; 3 news
- information officielle = judicial inquiry
- les faits qui résultent des informations = the facts established by the inquiry
- ouvrir une information = to start an preliminary investigation; to begin legal proceedings
- prendre des informations sur quelqu'un = to make inquiries about someone
informatique *adj & f* 1 computer *adj*; 2 computer science; computing; information technology
- effraction informatique = computer hacking
informer *v* inform (to); tell (to); inquire into (to) (eg crime); investigate (to) (eg crime)
- informer contre quelqu'un = to inform against someone; to start inquiries concerning someone
- informer sur un crime = to investigate a crime
infraction *f* offence; infringement; infraction
- auteur d'une infraction = offender
- commettre une infraction = to commit an offence
- être en infraction = to be committing an offence
- infraction à la loi = breaking the law
- infraction à un ordre = violation of an order
- infraction de droits = infringement of rights
- infraction pénale = criminal offence
- votre voiture stationne en infraction = your vehicle is illegally parked
inhabile *adj* unfitted; incapable; inept; clumsy
- inhabile à tester = incompetent to make a will
inhabilité *f* legal incapacity; disability
- inhabilité à succéder = incompetency to succeed
- inhabilité du mineur à tester = incapacity of a minor to make a will

inhabiliter *v* disqualify (to)
- inhabiliter quelqu'un à faire quelque chose = to disqualify someone from doing something
injonction *f* injunction
- injonction de payer = order / injunction to pay
- injonction thérapeutique = probation order with condition of attendance on a drug rehabilitation course
injure *f* abuse; insult; injury; tort
- bordée d'injures = string of abuse or insults
- être inculpé d'injure à quelqu'un = to be charged with abusing someone
- injure grave = serious injury or slander
- l'injure et la diffamation = abuse and slander
innocent,-e *adj*; **innocent** *m*, **innocente** *f* 1 innocent *adj*; 2 innocent person; simpleton
innocenter *v* clear (to); prove innocent (to)
- innocenter quelqu'un d'une accusation = to clear someone of a charge
inobservation *f* non-observance; inobservance; failure to observe (orders, etc)
inobservé,-e *adj* unobserved; not observed (rules, etc)
inopposabilité *f* non-invocability
inopposable *adj* incontestable; that cannot be opposed; non-invocable
inquisitoire *adj* inquisitorial
- procédure inquisitoire = proceedings under an interrogating judge
insaisissabilité *f* non-seizability; immunity from seizure or distraint
insaisissable *adj* not distrainable; non-seizable
inscription* *f* inscription; enrolment; registration
- feuille d'inscription = entry form
- inscription de faux = challenge (to the validity of a document); plea of forgery
- inscription hypothécaire = registration of a mortgage
- propriété libre de toute inscription = unencumbered estate
inscrire *v* note down (to); write down (to); register (to); enrol (to)
- s'incrire en faux = to lodge a challenge; to dispute the validity of

instance *f* legal proceedings; authority
- acquitté en seconde instance = acquitted on appeal
- affaire en instance = case on the cause list
- demande introductive d'instance = statement of claim
- introduire une instance = to institute legal proceedings
- les instances internationales = the international authorities
- pièces en instance = documents relating to the case (before court)
- tribunal d'instance = magistrates court

instituer *v* institute (to); establish (to); introduce (to) (eg tax); appoint (to) (heir, official, etc)
- instituer des poursuites contre quelqu'un = to institute proceedings against someone
- instituer quelqu'un héritier = to appoint someone as one's heir
- instituer une enquête = to institute an inquiry

institution *f* institution; private school; appointing (of heir)

instructeur *adj* examining
- juge / magistrat instructeur = examining magistrate

instruction *f* education; directive; instruction; investigation
- code d'instruction criminelle = code of criminal procedure
- instruction écrite = written statement of case
- juge d'instruction = examining magistrate
- ouvrir une instruction = to open an investigation or judicial inquiry

instruire *v* inform (to); teach (to); instruct (to); examine (to); investigate (to) (a case)
- instruire contre quelqu'un = to make investigations concerning someone

instrumenter *v* draw up a document or deed (to)
- instrumenter contre quelqu'un = to order proceedings to be taken against someone

intenter *v* **(une action, un procès à, contre quelqu'un)** bring (to) (an action); institute proceedings (to) (against someone)

- intenter une action en justice = to bring proceedings; to go to court

intention *f* intention
- avec intention de nuire = with malice
- dans l'intention de nuire = maliciously
- intention criminelle = mens rea

interdiction *f* interdiction; banning of; ban on
- demande en interdiction = petition that a spendthrift be deprived of financial control of his estate
- interdiction = state of minority declared by a court
- interdiction = deprival of control over money
- interdiction de séjour = prohibition from entering certain areas
- interdiction des droits civiques / civils / de famille = deprival of civic / civil / family rights
- interdiction légale = suspension of a convict's civic rights

intéressement *m* profit sharing (scheme)

interjection *f* lodging of an appeal; interjection
- interjection d'appel = lodging of an appeal

interjeter *v* **appel** lodge an appeal (to)

interlocuteur *m*, **interlocutrice** *f* 1 speaker; person; 2 negotiator; 3 representative
- interlocuteur valable = authorized representative

interposition *f* interposition; intervention; fraudulent use of a third party's identity as one's own

interrogatoire *m* interrogation; cross-examination
- contre-interrogatoire = cross-examination
- interrogatoire principal du témoin = principal examination of the witness
- nouvel interrogatoire = re-examination

interroger *v* interrogate (to); question (to)

interruption *f* interruption
- interruption de prescription = interruption of prescription
- interruption volontaire de grossesse (IVG) = termination of pregnancy

intervenant *m*, **intervenante** *f* intervener; intermediate; contributor; participant

intervenir *v* intervene (to); be reached (to) (eg agreement)
- intervenir à un contrat = to intervene in, or become a third party to, an agreement

intervention *f* intervention; becoming a third party in a contract, etc
- offre d'intervention = offer of mediation
- paiement par intervention = payment on behalf of a third party

intestat *adj* intestate
- décéder intestat = to die intestate
- hériter ab intestat = to succeed to an intestate estate
- mourir intestat = to die intestate

intimation *f* summons (before an appeal court); notification;
- faire des intimations aux partis = to summon the parties
- intimation = notice of appeal
- intimation de vider les lieux = notice to quit

intimé *m*, **intimée** *f* respondent; appellee; defendant (before Appeal Court)

intimer *v* summon (to) (before an Appeal Court); notify (to)
- faire intimer un appel à quelqu'un = to give someone notice of appeal
- intimer à quelqu'un l'ordre de partir = to give someone notice to go

intimidation *f* intimidation

intransmissibilité *f* intransmissibility; non-transferability

intransmissible *adj* intransmissible; non-transferable

introduire *v* introduce (to); insert (to); institute (to)
- introduire une instance = to institute legal proceedings; to present a plea

invalide *adj* disabled; invalid (eg will); null and void

invalider *v* invalidate (to)

invalidité *f* disability
- invalidité permanente = permanent disability; chronic ill-health
- pension d'invalidité = industrial disablement benefit

inventaire *m* inventory; stocklist; valuation (of investments, securities, etc)
- accepter une succession sous bénéfice d'inventaire = to accept an estate

without liability to debts beyond the descended assets
- faire / dresser un inventaire = to make an inventory
- faire l'inventaire de = to make an assessment of
- sous bénéfice d'inventaire = under beneficium inventori; conditionally, with reservations

inventer *v* invent (to); devise (to); find (to) (lost object, treasure etc)

inventeur *m*, **inventrice** *f* inventor; finder (of lost object, treasure, etc)

invention *f* invention; inventiveness; finding (of lost object, treasure, etc)
- brevet d'invention = patent (for an invention)
- invention d'un trésor = finding of treasure trove

inventorier *v* make an inventory of (to); make a stocklist of (to); inventory (to)

investir *v* vest (to); invest (to)
- capitaux investis = funded capital
- être investi d'un droit = to be vested with a right

invoquer *v* invoke (to); call upon (to) (witness); cite (to); refer to (to) (law, text)
- documents invoqués dans un litige = documents invoked in a suit
- invoquer le témoignage de quelqu'un = to call someone to witness
- invoquer les règles de compétence = to invoke the rules of jurisdiction
- les arguments de fait et de droit invoqués = the points of fact and law cited

irrecevable *adj* inadmissible
- être déclaré irrecevable en son action = to be non-suited
- témoignage irrecevable = inadmissible evidence

irréfragable *adj* irrebuttable; undeniable

irréfutable *adj* irrefutable; indisputable

irrégulier,-ière *adj* irregular; uneven
- absence irrégulière = unauthorized absence

irresponsabilité *f* non-accountability; irresponsability
- irresponsabilité pénale = criminal irresponsability

irrévocabilité *f* irrevocability
itératif,-ive *adj* iterative; reiterated; repeated
ivresse *f* intoxication
- conduite en état d'ivresse = drunken driving
- en état d'invresse publique = drunk and disorderly

J

jargon *m* jargon; slang
- jargon du palais = jargon of the law courts; legal jargon
- jargon juridique / médical / publicitaire = legal / medical / advertising jargon
jonction *f* junction; joining; joinder
- jonction d'instance = joinder
jouissance *f* enjoyment; use; possession of; tenure
- avoir la jouissance de certains droits = to enjoy certain rights
- date de jouissance = due date
- jouissance en commun (d'un bien) = communal tenure
- multijouissance = time-share
- privation de jouissance = deprivation of use of (eg property)
jour *m* day
- ce jour d'hui = this day
- jour-amende *m* = a daily based fine
- jour d'audience = court day
- jour férié = bank holiday
- jour ouvrable = working day
- par jour de retard = on a daily basis
judiciaire *adj* legal; judicial
- casier judiciaire = criminal record; police record
- contrôle judiciaire = judicial supervision
- enquête judiciaire = judicial enquiry
- erreur judiciaire = miscarriage of justice
- frais judiciaires = legal charges
- vente judiciaire = sale by court order
juge *m* judge
- juge aux affaires familiales = judge dealing with family affairs

- juge aux affaires matrimoniales = divorce court judge
- juge d'instance = magistrate; justice of the peace
- juge d'instruction = examining judge or magistrate
- juge de l'application des peines = judge appointed to oversee conditions of a prisoner's sentence
- juge de paix = justice of the peace
- juge des enfants = judge hearing cases involving minors
- juge des référés = judge sitting in Chambers
- juge des tutelles = judge administering the property of persons under guardianship
- juge du fond = judge in the lower courts
- juge unique = single judge
- oui, Monsieur le juge = yes, Your Honour
jugeable *adj* subject to judgement in court
- difficilement jugeable = difficult to judge
jugement *m* judgment; trial; sentence (criminal case); decision; award (civil case)
- confirmer un jugement en appel = to uphold / affirm a judgement
- déférer pour jugement = to commit for trial
- détention sans jugement = detention without trial
- faire passer / mettre quelqu'un en jugement = to bring someone to trial
- jugement attaqué = decision challenged
- jugement contradictoire = judgment after trial
- jugement déclaratif de décès = declaratory judgement of death / demise
- jugement déclaratif de faillite = adjudication in bankruptcy
- jugement déclaratoire = declaratory judgment
- jugement définitif = final judgement; decree absolute
- jugement en constatation de paternité = affiliation order
- jugement exécutoire par provision = judgment provisionally enforceable
- jugement mis en délibéré = reserved judgement

- jugement par défaut = judgment by default
- jugement provisoire = decree nisi
- jugement sur le fond = judgement pronounced on the merits
- le tribunal est en jugement = the court is sitting
- modifier un jugement en appel = to vary a judgement
- passer en jugement = to stand trial
- poursuivre quelqu'un en jugement = to take legal proceedings against someone; to sue someone
- prononcer / rendre un jugement = to pass judgment / sentence
- rendre un jugement = to deliver / pronounce judgement

juger *v* judge (to); try (to); adjudicate (to)
- être jugé pour meurtre = to be tried for murder
- juger un procès = to judge / try a case
- juger une réclamation / un différend = to adjudicate a claim / dispute
- le jury a jugé qu'elle n'était pas coupable = the jury found her not guilty

juré *m* juror

juridiction *f* jurisdiction; courts
- juridiction civile = civil courts
- juridiction collégiale = court where cases are heard by at least three judges
- juridiction commerciale = commercial court
- juridiction consulaire = commercial court
- juridiction d'exception = court of limited jurisdiction
- juridiction d'instruction = pre-trial investigation court
- juridiction de droit commun = court with general jurisdiction
- juridiction de jugement = trial court
- juridiction de simple police = magistrate's courts; police courts
- juridiction du premièr degré = first instance court
- juridiction échevinale = court composed of both career judges and lay judges
- juridiction judiciaire = ordinary court
- juridiction locale = local court
- juridiction pénale = criminal court
- juridiction répressive = criminal court

- juridiction sociale = industrial tribunal
- saisir une juridiction = to refer a case to court

juridique *adj* juridicial; judicial; legal
- conseiller juridique = legal adviser
- frais juridiques = lawyer's fees; legal charges (incurred in a transaction)

jurisprudence *f* jurisprudence; statute law; case law

jury *m* jury
- chef du jury = foreman of the jury
- constituer un jury = to empanel a jury
- dresser la liste du jury = to empanel the jury
- exercer fonction de jury = to do jury service
- membre du jury = member of the jury; juror
- président du jury = foreman of the jury

justice *f* justice
- agir en justice = sue (to)
- déni de justice = miscarriage of justice
- Palais de Justice = Law Courts
- palais de justice = courthouse
- se faire justice = (of murderer) to commit suicide

justiciable *adj & m,f* 1 justiciable; answerable; 2 person subject to trial; 3 litigant
- criminel justiciable de la Cour d'assises = criminal subject to the criminal court
- justiciable d'un tribunal = justiciable to a court; subject to the jurisdiction of a court
- les justiciables = those up for trial; those within jurisdiction (of court)

justicier *m*, **justicière** *f* upholder of the law; dispenser of justice; judge

L

laisser *v* leave (to); let (to); allow (to)
- laisser un enfant à ses parents = to leave a child in the custody of his / her parents

ledit *m*; **ladite** *f*; **lesdit(e)s** *pl adj* (see also

audit, dudit) the aforementioned; the aforesaid (in legal documents)

légal,-e *adj* legal; lawful; statutory
- avoir recours aux moyens légaux = to have recourse to the law; to institute legal proceedings
- médicine légale = forensic medicine
- par voies légaux = by legal process

légataire *m,f* legatee; devisee; heir
- légataire à titre particulier = specific legatee; beneficiary of specific amount or specific asset
- légataire à titre universel = beneficiary of a proportion of an estate
- légataire universel = universal or residuary legatee

légitimation *f* legitimation (eg of child); official recognition

légitime *adj* 1 legitimate; lawful; 2 justifiable
- cas de légitime défense = case of self-defence
- descendant légitime = legitimate descendent
- enfant légitime / illégitime = legitimate / illegitimate child
- héritier légitime = rightful heir
- propriétaire légitime = legal owner

légitimement *adv* legitimately; lawfully; rightfully

légitimité *f* legitimacy

legs *m* legacy; bequest
- caducité du legs = lapsing of a legacy
- faire un legs à quelqu'un = to leave a legacy to someone
- legs (à titre) particulier = legacy of one or more specifically designated items of property
- legs à titre universel = proportional share of legacy (ie of disposable quota); residue of the estate
- legs caduc = null and void legacy
- legs (de biens mobiliers) = legacy
- legs (de terres, de biens immobiliers) = devise; legacy of real property
- legs de residuo = life interest in a bequest
- legs universel = universal bequest (where legacy is the totality of estate or disposable quota)

léguer *v* bequeath (to); devise (to)

léser *v* wrong (to); damage (to); injure (to)
- la partie lésée = the injured party
- léser les droits de quelqu'un = to infringe on someone's rights

lésion *f* lesion; injury; wrong
- contrat où il y a lésion = burdensome contract
- lésions internes = internal injuries

levé *m* survey
- un levé de terrain = a land survey

levée *f* raising; lifting; levying (eg tax)
- levée d'écrou = release from prison
- levée de jugement = transcipt (of a verdict)
- levée de quarantaine = lifting of quarantine
- levée des scellés = removal of the seals

lever *v* lift (to); raise (to); levy (to); exercise (to); take up (to) (eg option)
- lever l'option = to accept the offer to sell by the vendor
- lever les scellés = to remove the seals
- lever une quarantaine = to lift a quarantine
- lever une saisie = to lift an embargo

liberalité *f* liberality; gift

libération *f* liberation; release
- faire bénéficier d'une libération conditionnelle = to release on parole
- libération conditionnelle = release on parole

libérer *v* free (to); release (to); decontrol (to) (eg prices)
- être libéré sous caution / sur parole = to be released on bail / on parole
- libérer un garant = to discharge a surety
- libérer un prisonnier = to release a prisoner

liberté *f* liberty; freedom
- être en liberté = to be free
- être mis en liberté provisoire = to be released on bail; to be granted bail
- être mis en liberté surveillée = to be put on probation
- liberté d'expression = freedom of speech
- libertés publiques = civil liberties
- mettre en liberté conditionnelle = to release on parole

- mettre en liberté sous caution = to release on bail
- mise en liberté = discharge or release (of prisoner)
- semi-liberté = relative freedom; partial release

libre *adj* free; unrestricted
- avoir la libre disposition de ses biens = to have free disposal of one's property / goods

licence *f* licence; permit; degree (eg of a university)
- détenteur d'une licence = licensee
- licence d'importation / d'exportation = import / export licence
- licence de débitant = licence to sell beer, wines and spirits
- licence de fabrication = manufacturing licence

licencié *m*, **licenciée** *f* licensee; permit-holder; graduate (of a university)

licenciement *m* dismissal (of employee)
- licenciement abusif = unfair dismissal
- licenciement fautif = wrongful dismissal
- licenciement justifié = fair dismissal
- préavis de licenciement = notice of dismissal

licencier *v* dismiss (to) (employee)

licitation *f* sale by auction in one lot of property held in indivision

lien *m* bond; link; tie
- lien de parenté = family relationship; blood tie
- lien du sang = blood tie

lier *v* bind (to); tie (to)

liquidateur *m*, **liquidatrice** *f* liquidator; receiver
- liquidateur judiciaire ; liquidateur de faillite = official liquidator / receiver
- placer une entreprise entre les mains d'un liquidateur = to put a company into receivership

liquidation *f* **judiciaire** compulsory liquidation

liquider *v* liquidate (to); wind up (to) (eg business, company); settle (to) (eg succession, debt, account); sell off (to)

liquidité *f* liquidity
- liquidités = liquid assets

lit *m* bed

- les enfants d'un autre lit = the children of a previous marriage
- les enfants du premier / deuxième lit = the children of the first / second marriage

litige *m* dispute; litigation; lawsuit
- être en litige = to be in dispute; to be in litigation
- les parties en litige = the litigants
- objet de litige = subject of the action / contention

local *m*, **locaux** *mpl* premises; building; accomodation unit; room
- local à usage commercial = shop; commercial premises
- local commercial; rez commercial = business premises
- local d'habitation = dwelling; residential unit; domestic premises
- locaux = offices; premises
- locaux insalubres = buildings unfit for habitation; insanitary buildings
- taxe sur les locaux loués meublés = tax on property rented furnished

locataire *m* & *f* 1 lessee; leaseholder; tenant; 2 lodger; 3 renter; hirer
- locataire à bail = lessee; leaseholder
- sous-locataire = sub-lessee

locataire *m,f* **à bail** lessee

locateur *m*; **locatrice** *f* lessor

locatif, locative *adj* relating to renting of premises
- impôts locatifs = rates
- prix locatif = rent
- réparations locatives = repairs incumbent on the tenant
- risques locatifs = tenant's risks
- valeur locative = rental value

location *f* hiring; letting (eg house); renting; tenancy
- agent de location = house agent
- location-accession = lease with an option to purchase
- location-bail = lease; leasing; leasehold
- location d'immeubles = house letting; flat letting
- location de logements = letting (residential) accommodation
- location saisonnière = holiday letting
- location-vente = hire purchase; purchase by instalments

- prix de location = rent

logement *m* dwelling house; accommodation; apartment; lodging
- indemnité de logement = housing allowance
- logement achevé = completed house
- logement en copropriété = apartment block
- logement neuf = new house / apartment

loi *f* law
- loi pénale = criminal law
- loi sur la presse = law preventing monopoly of the press

lot *m* share of estate; portion; condominium unit

lotir *v* divide into lots (to); divide up (to); share out (to) (eg estate)
- lotir terrain = to divide into plots
- lotir une propriété = to parcel out an estate

lotissement *m* housing estate or site; housing development; allotment; building plot; dividing into lots; parcelling out;

louage *m* letting; hiring
- contrat de louage d'ouvrage = contract for services
- louage d'immeubles = house letting; flat letting

loyer *m* rent; rental
- donner à loyer = to let
- loyer arrière = back rent
- prendre une maison à loyer = to rent a house

lu et approuvé, bon pour accord read, approved and agreed (endorsement with signature on a legal document)

M

magistrat *m* magistrate
- magistrat de carrière = career judge
- magistrat de l'instruction = examining magistrate
- magistrat du parquet = magistrate attached to Public Prosecutor's office; public prosecutor

- magistrat instructeur = examining magistrate
- magistrats "du siege" = judges
- outrage à magistrat = contempt of court

magistrature *f* magistracy; magistrature
- entrer dans la magistrature = to be appointed judge or public prosecutor
- la magistrature assise = the judges; the Bench
- la magistrature debout = the public prosecutors

mainlevée *f* withdrawal
- accorder mainlevée d'une saisie = to grant replevin
- mainlevée d'hypothèque = release of mortgage
- mainlevée de saisie = replevin; restoration of goods; cancellation of garnishee order

mainmise *f* seizure; distraint; takeover

maintien *m* maintenance; keeping

mairie *f* office of the mayor; local administrative office; town hall; council offices

maison *f* house; home
- maison centrale = prison
- maison d'arrêt = prison
- maison de correction = reformatory; reform prison
- maison de redressement = reformatory

maître *m* master; (title of address given to lawyers, notaires, etc)
- maître d'école = primary school teacher; schoolmaster
- maître de l'ouvrage = (privé) employer; (public) contracting authority
- maître en droit = law degree (approx. equivalent to LL.B)

majeur,-e *adj & m,f* 1 major; of age *adj*; 2 person who is of age (18 years or over)
- devenir majeur / majeure = to attain one's majority; to come of age
- il n'est pas encore majeur = he has not reached 18 yet
- majeur protégé = a (legally) protected major

majorité *f* majority
- atteindre sa majorité = to attain one's majority; to come of age

maladie *f* sickness; illness; disease

- assurance maladie = health insurance
- caisse de maladie = sick benefit insurance
- congé (de) maladie = sick leave
- maladie professionnelle = industrial disease
- prestation-maladie = sick benefit
- simuler une maladie = to feign illness; to malinger

malfaçon f 1 fault; defect (due to poor workmanship); 2 malpractice; cheating

malfaiteur m criminal
- association de malfaiteurs = criminal conspiracy

malveillance f malevolence; spite; foul play
- agir sans malveillance = to act without malicious intent
- avec malveillance = malevolently

mandant m, mandante f mandator; principal (in a transaction); employer

mandat m 1 power of attorney; proxy; 2 mandate; warrant; 3 money order; 4 agency agreement
- décerner un mandat d'arrêt = to issue an arrest warrant
- mandat ad litem = power of attorney
- mandat d'amener = order to offender or witness to appear (enforceable by arrest); summons
- mandat d'arrêt = arrest warrant
- mandat d'expulsion = eviction order
- mandat de comparution = summons (to appear); subpoena
- mandat de dépôt = committal order (of prisoner)
- mandat de perquisition = search warrant
- mandat exclusif = exclusive selling order (single agent)
- mandat international = international money order
- mandat simple = non-exclusive selling order (two or more agents)

mandataire m,f proxy; attorney; assignee; authorized agent; representative
- les avocats sont les mandataires légaux des plaideurs = lawyers are the legal representatives of litigants
- mandataire liquidateur m = liquidator, receiver

mandement m mandate; mandamus order; subpoena

manifestation f demonstration

manquement m 1 lack; 2 breach; failure; omission; lapse
- manqement à des obligations contractuelles = default
- manquement à l'obligation de prudence = negligence
- manquement à une règle = breach / violation of a rule
- manquement au devoir de probité = breach of probity / integrity
- manquement aux devoirs de la profession = unprofessional conduct

marc m mark
- au marc le franc = pro rata; proportionally
- marc le franc = pro rata repartition (of assets)

marchandage m bargaining; haggling; illegal subcontracting of labour

marchander v 1 haggle over (to); bargain over (to); 2 subcontract (to)

marchandeur m, marchandeuse f 1 haggler; 2 subcontractor (of labour)

marché m 1 market; 2 deal; bargain; contract
- arrêter un marché = to conclude a bargain
- marché à terme = settlement bargain; settlement market
- marché ferme = firm bargain; firm deal
- passer un marché = to enter into a bargain

mariage m marriage
- acte de mariage = marriage certificate
- contrat de mariage = pre-marital agreement; marriage settlement
- mariage blanc = sham marriage; unconsummated marriage
- mariage brisé = broken down marriage
- mettre opposition à mariage = to lodge objection to a marriage
- nullité du mariage = nullity (of marriage)
- promesse de mariage = promise of marriage
- rupture de promesse de mariage = breach of promise of marriage
- violation de promesse de mariage = breach of promise

marital,-e *adj* marital
- autorisation maritale = husband's authorization

masse *f* mass; fund; prisoner's earnings (handed over to him / her on release)
- masse active = assets
- masse de recourse = emergency fund
- masse des biens = total estate; assets
- masse des créanciers = general body of creditors
- masse passive = liabilities
- plan de masse = overall plan (surveying)

maternité *f* maternity
- congé de maternité = maternity leave

matière *f* matter; material; subject matter; field; area
- arbitrage en matière de salaire = wage arbitration
- compétence en matière civile / pénale = civil / criminal jurisdiction
- matière contentieuse = contentious matter
- matière prud'homale = matters heard by the Conseil des Prud'Hommes
- matières sommaires = summary matters

maximum *adj & m* 1 maximum *adj*; 2 maximum; maximum sentence

mémoire *f* 1 memory; 2 memorandum; statement of case; report
- présenter une mémoire = to give a detailed account (eg of costs)

menace *f* threat; menace; intimidation
- lettre des menaces = threatening letter
- menaces = intimidation; threats
- menaces de part et d'autre = threats and counterthreats
- menaces de voies de fait = assault
- recevoir des menaces de mort = to receive death threats

méprise *f* mistake
- par méprise = by mistake; inadvertently

mère *f* mother
- mère adoptive = adoptive mother; foster mother
- mère célibataire = single mother
- mère de famille = mother; housewife
- mère porteuse = surrogate mother

message *m* message

meuble *m* (also *adj*) piece of furniture; movable

- biens meubles = movables; personal estate; chattels; personalty
- faire la liste des meubles = to make a list or inventory of the furniture
- le meuble = furniture
- meubles meublants = furniture; movables

meurtre *m* murder
- être jugé pour meurtre = to be tried for murder
- tentative de meurtre = attempted murder

mineur,-e *adj*; **mineur** *m,f* 1 minor; under age *adj*; 2 minor; young person under 18
- enfant mineur = minor
- être mineur = to be under age
- mineurs délinquants = juvenile delinquents
- plaider l'incapacité en tant que mineur = to plead infancy

minimum *adj & m*, **minimums** *pl*, **minima** *pl* 1 minimum *adj*; 2 minimum; minimum sentence
- minimum viellesse = basic old age pension
- minimum vital = minimum living wage

minorité *f* minority; (legal) infancy; nonage
- appuyer sa défense sur sa minorité = to plead infancy
- minorité pénale = legal infancy
- pendant sa minorité = while under age; during his / her infancy

minute *f* minute; moment; minute (written record); draft of a contract
- les minutes de la réunion = the minutes of the meeting

minuter *v* time (to); draw up (to); draft (to)
- emploi du temps minuté = use of a strict schedule or timetable

mise *f* **en demeure** summons or formal notice (to do something); formal demand

mise *f* **en état** pre-trial stage in civil proceedings

mise *f* **en œuvre** 1 implementation; implementing (regulation); 2 using; marshalling; employing 3 construction; workmanship

mitigation *f* mitigation

mitoyenneté *f* common ownership (eg of a wall, fence)

mobilier,-ière *adj*; **mobilier** *m* 1 movable; transferable; 2 furniture; personal property; movable property
- biens mobiliers = personal estate; chattels; personalty
- saisie mobilière = seizure of movable property

modalité *f* mode; method; modality; means; way; (restrictive) clause
- modalité d'application de la loi = mode of enforcing the law
- modalités de mise en œuvre = details of implementation, operating conditions
- modalités de paiement = methods / terms of payment
- modalités d'une entente = ways for reaching an understanding / agreement

mode *m* form; mode; method

modération *f* moderation; restraint; reduction
- apporter les modérations à un impôt = to reduce a tax
- modération de peine = mitigation of penalty

mœurs *fpl* morals; manners; customs
- affaire de mœurs = sex case
- mœurs spéciales = homosexual practices

montant *m* total amount; (sum) total
- montant compensatoire = subsidy
- montant de la demande = amount claimed
- montant dû = outstanding amount
- montant forfaitaire = lump um
- montant net d'une succession = residuary estate
- montant nominal = par value

moratoire *adj & m*; **moratorium** *m* 1 moratory *adj*; 2 moratorium
- intérêts moratoires = interest on payments overdue

morceler *v* parcel out (to)

motif *m* motive; ground; reason for the decision; motif; pattern
- au motif de = on the ground of
- motifs d'un jugement = grounds upon which a judgement has been made

motiver *v* give reasons (to)

moyen *m* means; ground
- moyen de défense = ground for defence

- moyen de pression = means of applying pressure

mur *m* wall
- être propriétaire des murs = to own the premises

mutabilité *f* mutability; alienability

mutable *adj* changeable; mutable; alienable

mutation *f* transfer (eg of ownership, property); transformation; mutation
- impôt sur les mutations = tax on property transfers
- mutation entre vifs = property transfer inter vivos

N

nantir *v* secure (to) (eg a creditor)
- nantir une hypothèque = to register a mortgage
- se nantir de = to secure oneself with; to provide oneself with
- se nantir des effets d'une succession = to secure an inheritance by taking possession

nantissement *m* security; hypothecation; pledge; collateral security
- déposer des titres en nantissement = to lodge stock as a security
- droit de nantissement = lien on goods
- nantissement du prix = purchase price guaranteed

nationalité *f* nationality
- certificate de nationalité française = certificate of French nationality
- déchéance de nationalité = loss or withdrawal of nationality
- nationalité d'origine = original nationality

négligence *f* negligence; carelessness
- négligence coupable; négligence criminelle = criminal negligence
- négligence grave; grosse négligence = gross negligence

négociation *f* negotiation

négocier *v* negotiate (to)

nier *v* deny (to); repudiate (to)
- nier un fait = to deny

- nier une allégation de fait = to traverse; to deny an allegation of fact
- nier une dette = to repudiate a debt

nommer *v* appoint (to)

non-assistance *f* non-assistance
- non-assistance à personne en danger = failure to give assistance to a person in danger

non-comparution *f* nonappearance; failure to appear in court

non-jouissance *f* nonenjoyment; prevention of possession

non-lieu *m* no ground for prosecution; no true bill
- bénéficier d'un non-lieu = to be discharged; to have one's case dismissed for lack of evidence
- ordonnance de non-lieu = nonsuit

non-rétroactivité *f* nonretroactivity

non-valeur *f* object of no value; worthless security; bad debt; non-productive land etc

nonobstant *prep & adv* 1 notwithstanding *prep*; despite; in spite of; 2 notwithstanding *adv*; nevertheless *adv*
- ce nonobstant = this notwithstanding
- nonobstant toute clause contraire = notwithstanding any clause to the contrary

norme *f* legal norm

notaire *m* notary; notary public; solicitor (conveyancing)

notification *f* notification; notice
- notification d'actes = service of documents
- recevoir notification de = to be notified of

novation *f* 1 novation; substitution (of a new obligation for a previous one); 2 renewal (eg of lease)

nu-propriétaire *m*, **nue-propriétaire** *f* owner without usufruct; bare owner

nue-propriété *f* ownership without usufruct
- avoir un bien en nue-propriété = to have a property without usufruct

nuire *v* be injurious to (to); harm (to); prejudice (to)
- dans l'intention de nuire = maliciously
- nuire aux intérêts de quelqu'un = to prejudice someone's interests

nul, nulle *adj* nil; null and void; non-existant
- déclarer un décret nul et non avenu = to annul a decree
- rendre nul = to annul; to nullify

nullité *f* nullity; invalidity (eg of marriage, deed); incompetence
- action en nullité = action for avoidance of contract
- cession atteinte de nullité = invalid assignment
- frapper un clause de nullité = to render a clause void
- nullité absolue = absolute nullity
- nullité du mariage = invalidity of the marriage
- nullité du testament; nullité du legs = invalidity of the will
- nullité relative = relative nullity

O

objection *f* objection
- faire / formuler / soulever une objection = to raise / make an objection
- répondre à une objection = to meet an objection; to dispose of an objection

objet *m* object; purpose
- l'objet d'un litige = the subject of an action; the matter at issue
- objet de la demande = statement of claim
- objet du litige = points at issue
- objet immobilier = realty
- objet mobilier = personalty
- objets de valeur = valuables
- objets litigieux = goods in dispute

obligation *f* obligation; duty; recognizance; bond; debenture
- contracter une obligation irrévocable = to enter into a binding agreement
- faillir à ses obligations = to fail to meet one's obligations
- inexécution d'une obligation contractuelle = default of contractual obligation
- manquement à l'obligation de prudence = negligence

ordonnance

- obligation alimentaire = maintenance order
- obligation contractuelle = privity in deed
- obligation d'entretien = obligation to maintain in good repair (flat, house)
- obligation de vigilance = duty of care
- obligation des parents = parental duties
- obligation exécutoire = operative obligation
- obligation légale = legal obligation
- obligation morale = moral obligation
- obligation solidaire = obligation binding on all parties

obligatoire *adj* obligatory; mandatory; compulsory
- décision obligatoire pour tous = decision binding on all parties

obligé,-e *adj & m,f* 1 obliged; compelled; required; 2 obligee; debtor

obliger *v* oblige (to); bind (to); compel (to)

occupant *m*, **occupante** *f* occupier; occupant
- avoué occupant = solicitor in charge of a case
- le premier occupant = the first occupier
- occupant de bonne foi = occupier (without a lease)

occupation *f* occupation; occupancy (eg of house); job; employment
- occupation de fait de la maison d'autrui = squatting

octroi *m* granting; concession
- conditions d'octroi = conditions for granting

œuvres *fpl* **sociales** company benefit scheme

officier *m* **de police judiciaire (OPJ)** = senior police officer

officine *f* dispensary; pharmacy (technical and legal term for)

offrant *m* bidder; offerer
- le plus offrant = the highest bidder

offre *f* offer
- offre d'intervention = offer of mediation
- une offre réelle = tender money in discharge of a debt

opposabilité *f* opposability

opposant,-e *adj* opposing
- la partie opposante; la partie adverse = the opposing party

opposition *f* opposition
- agir en opposition avec un droit = to act in contravention of a right
- faire opposition à un chèque = to stop payment of a cheque
- faire opposition à une décision / un jugement = to appeal against
- jugement susceptible d'opposition = judgment liable to stay of execution
- mettre opposition à mariage = to lodge objection to a marriage
- opposition à paiement = payment objection (lodged by an unpaid creditor against payment being made to a debtor)

option *f* option

ordinaire *adj & m* 1 ordinary; normal; 2 custom; usual practice
- régler une affaire à l'ordinaire = to refer a case from the criminal to the civil courts

ordonnance *f* prescription; order; (judge's) order; judgment; ruling
- ordonnance d'adoption = adoption order
- ordonnance d'assistance = care order
- ordonnance de clôture = order to terminate the 'mise en état'
- ordonnance de divorce = decree of divorce
- ordonnance de garde conjointe = split order (custody to one parent, care and control to other)
- ordonnance de mise sous séquestre = writ of seqestration; receiving order (in bankruptcy case)
- ordonnance de non-lieu = order of no case to answer
- ordonnance de référé = order delivered by judge sitting in Chambers; provisional order; injunction
- ordonnance de renvoi = committal for trial
- ordonnance de saisie de biens immobiliers = writ of possession
- ordonnance de saisie-exécution = writ of execution
- ordonnance de saisie mobilière = writ of fieri facias
- ordonnance de séparation = judicial separation order
- ordonnance de surseoir = stay of

execution
- rendre une ordonnance = to make an order

ordonner *v* 1 arrange (to); organize (to); 2 order (to); 3 ordain (to) (priest)

ordre *m* order
- à l'ordre de = to the order of (cheque, etc)
- ordre d'achat = buying order; order to buy
- ordre de juridiction = system of courts
- ordre de succession = order of distribution (when person dies intestate)
- ordre de vente = selling order; order to sell
- ordre du jour = agenda
- Ordre des Architectes = Association of Architects
- Ordre des Avocats = Association of Barristers
- ordre des descendants / héritiers = order of descent

organique *adj* organic

origine *f* origin; source; birth; nationality
- certificat d'origine = certificate of origine
- d'origine = authentic; certified (document)
- origine de propriété = vendor's title to property

otage *m* hostage
- être pris en otage = to be taken hostage

ouïr *v* hear (to) (eg witness)

outrage *m* insult; outrage
- outrage à agent = insulting behaviour (to police officer)
- outrage à la pudeur = public act of indecency; indecent exposure
- outrage à magistrat = contempt of court
- outrage aux bonnes mœurs = affront to public decency; public act of indecency
- outrage aux mœurs = indecency

P

paisible *adj* peaceful; calm; quiet; untroubled

- possesseur paisible = uncontested owner

palais *m* palace; law courts
- le Palais = the law courts
- le palais de Justice = the law courts
- terme de palais = legal term; forensic term

par-devant *prep & adv* 1 before *prep*; 2 in front of; round the front *adv*
- acte signé par-devant notaire = deed signed in presence of a notaire

par-devers *prep* in the hands of; before
- par-devers le juge = before the judge
- retenir des papiers par-devers soi = to keep papers in one's possession

paraphe *m* paraph (ie flourish written under one's signature); initials (of one's name)

parapher *v* initial (to); sign one's initials on (to); sign (to)

parcelle *f* parcel (of land)
- parcelle de terre = plot of land

pardon *m* pardon; forgiveness; remission of a sentence
- pardon d'une offense conjugale = condonation

parent *m*, **parente** *f* parent; (blood) relation; relative
- parent isolé = lone parent; single parent
- parents adoptifs = adoptive parents
- parents naturels = natural parents
- parents nourriciers = foster parents
- plus proche parent = next of kin
- proche parent = relative
- sans parents = without parents; orphaned

paritaire *adj* with equal representation on both sides

parjure *adj & m,f* 1 perjured *adj*; 2 perjurer; 3 perjury
- commettre un parjure = to commit perjury

parquet *m* 1 public prosecutor's office or department; 2 well of court; 3 parquet floor
- le parquet = the prosecution

partage *m* division; sharing; partition (of real property); share; portion; lot
- donation-partage = partitition by gift
- partage d'une succession = division of an estate

- partages faits par les ascendants = partition of property by ascendants
- testament-partage = partition by will

participation f participation; sharing; profit sharing
- participation aux acquêts = sharing of property acquired in common by husband and wife
- participation aux bénéfices = profit sharing; participation in profits
- participation des ouvriers aux bénéfices = industrial partnership

particulier m private person; private individual
- particulier simple = private individual

partie f party (eg to a contract, a dispute); person signing a contract; litigant; part (of a whole)
- la partie adverse = the other side; the other party
- la partie lésée = the injured party; the aggrieved party
- les parties contractantes = the contracting parties
- les parties du contrat = the contracting parties
- partie civile = plaintiff / victim claiming damages (in a criminal case); claimant
- partie en cause = party to the case
- partie privative = flat in a block or in a house
- partie requérante = claimant
- parties communes = common parts (eg of block of flats)
- prise à partie = suing a magistrate for denial of justice
- se porter partie civile = to bring a civil action against someone

pas m **de porte** goodwill (of business); key money (flat)

passation f drawing up (of contract); signing (of agreement); entering into (contract, lease); entry (into accounts ledger); placing (of order); filing (of return at registration office)
- passation d'une commande = placing of an order
- passation de l'acte = signing the deed of sale
- passation de pouvoir = transmission of powers; take over

passavant m transire (customs permit); permit; carnet

passer* v pass (to); come up (to)
- acte passé devant un notaire = document drawn up before a notaire
- passer en justice = to come up before the courts
- passer un accord = to conclude an agreement
- passer un contrat = to sign a contract

paternité f paternity
- action en recherche de paternité = paternity suit
- confusion de part; confusion de paternité = doubt over paternity
- désaveu de paternité = repudiation of paternity; contestation of legitimacy
- jugement en constatation de paternité = affiliation order
- reconnaissance de paternité judiciaire = affiliation order

patrimoine m inheritance; heritage; patrimony; property; estate
- gestion de patrimoine = estate management; private assets management
- séparation des patrimoines = law under which the creditors of the diseased have prior claim on the estate

peine* f punishment; penalty; sentence
- dispense de peine = absolute discharge
- dispense de peine conditionnelle = conditional discharge
- peine alternative = alternative sentence
- peine capitale = capital punishment
- peine contractuelle = penalty for non-performance (of a contract)
- peine correctionnelle = sentence of two months to five years imprisonment
- peine criminelle = sentence for a serious crime
- peine de mort = death penalty
- peine de police = sentence of one day to two months imprisonment
- peine de prison = prison sentence; custodial sentence
- peine de substitution = alternative sentence
- peine incompressible = prison sentence

with no provision for remission
- peine non privative de liberté = non custodial sentence
- peine privative de liberté = custodial sentence
- prononcer une peine = to pass sentence
- remise de peine = remission of sentence

pendant,-e *adj* hanging; pending; outstanding
- procès pendant = pending action at law; pending lawsuit

pension *f* pension; allowance; alimony
- pension alimentaire = maintenance; financial allowance; financial provision; financial relief
- pension viagère = life annuity
- titre de pension = pension book

percevoir *v* 1 collect (to) (tax); receive (to) (eg pension, salary, rent); 2 perceive (to)

perdant *m* losing party (in a lawsuit)

père *m* father
- bon père de famille = prudent administrator (of family wealth); tenant taking good care of the rented property; responsible citizen
- M. Javin père = Mr. Javin senior
- valeurs de père de famille = gilt-edged securities

périmer *v* lapse (to); become out-of-date (to)
- laisser périmer un droit = to allow a right to lapse; to forfeit a right
- un billet périmé = an out-of-date ticket
- un passeport périmé = an expired passport

permis *m* permit; licence
- annulation du permis de conduire = removal of driving licence
- permis d'importation = import licence
- permis d'inhumer = burial certificate
- permis de conduire = driving licence; driving test
- permis de construire = building permit; planning permission
- permis de démolir = permit to demolish a building
- permis de port d'arme = gun licence
- permis de séjour = residence permit
- permis de travail = work permit
- retirer le permis de conduire = to

disqualify / ban from driving
- retrait du permis de conduire = disqualification from driving

perquisition *f* house search

personne *f* person; individual
- par personne interposée = through a third party / person
- passer par une tierce personne = to negotiate through a third party
- les droits de la personne = the rights of the individual
- personne à charge = dependent
- personne civile = legal entity
- personne déplacée = displaced person
- personne juridique = legal entity
- personne morale = legal entity (eg a company, a corporation)
- personne physique = individual
- personne qui occupe la maison d'autrui = squatter
- personne vulnérable = vulnerable person
- tierce personne = third party

personnel,-elle *adj* personal; non-transferable

pièce* *f* piece; paper; document; room
- pièce à conviction = exhibit (in a case)
- pièce annexe; pièce jointe = enclosure
- pièce d'identité = identity document
- pièce justificative = documentary proof or evidence
- pièces d'un procès = documents of a case

place *f* place; position
- à la place de = in lieu of
- droits de place = stall rent

placet *m* petition; claim (plaintiff's)

plaider *v* plead (to) (a cause); go to court (to); litigate (to)
- il aime à plaider = he is fond of litigation
- plaider contre quelqu'un = to take someone to court
- plaider coupable = to plead guilty
- plaider non coupable = to plead not guilty
- son défenseur va plaider la folie = his counsel will plead insanity

plaideur *m*, **plaideuse** *f* litigant; suitor; litigious person

plaidoirie *f* speech for the defence; address to the court; plea; appeal

plaidoyer *m* speech to the Court; speech for the defence; plea
- mon plaidoyer démontre que ... = my argument shows that ...

plaignant *m*, **plaignante** *f* plaintiff

plaindre (se) *v* make a complaint (to); complain (to)
- se plaindre de quelqu'un / quelque chose = to make complaint about someone / some thing

plainte *f* complaint
- plainte contre X = action against person or persons unknown
- porter plainte / donner plainte / déposer une plainte contre quelqu'un = to lodge a complaint against someone; to sue someone
- porter plainte en justice = to bring an action at law

pli* *m* letter; folded cover
- sous pli cacheté = in a sealed envelope
- sous pli separé = under separate cover
- un pli urgent = an urgent letter

plus-value *f* increase in value; increment value; appreciation; excess yield (of tax, etc)
- impôt sur les plus-values = capital gains tax

police *f* 1 police; police force; 2 policy (assurance, insurance)
- agent de police = police constable
- commissaire de police = superintendent of police
- comissariat de police = police station
- fonctionnaire de police = police officer
- maintenir la police de l'audience = to keep order during the court hearing
- police des mœurs; police mondaine = vice squad
- police judiciaire (PJ) = Criminal Investigation Dept. (CID)
- préfet de police = Commissioner; police chief
- détenteur d'une police = policy holder
- police automobile = car insurance policy
- police d'assurance contre l'incendie = fire insurance policy
- police multirisques habitation = building insurance policy

pornographique *adj* pornographic; obscene

possession *f* possession; ownership
- possession prolongée acquisitive = possession leading to ownership
- prendre possession d'un héritage = to come into one's inheritance

postérieur *adj* later; subsequent to (à)

postulation *f* right to represent (a client by a lawyer)

postuler *v* 1 apply for (to) (eg job); 2 postulate (to); 3 represent (to) (a client by a lawyer)

poursuite *f* 1 pursuit; chase; 2 lawsuit; action; prosecution; suing (of a debtor)
- commencer / engager / intenter des poursuites contre quelqu'un = to start legal proceedings against someone
- poursuites civiles / pénales = civil / criminal proceedings
- poursuites judiciaires = legal proceedings
- poursuites pénales = prosecution
- poursuites publiques = public prosecution
- s'exposer à des poursuites = to lay oneself open to prosecution

poursuivant,-e *adj*, **poursuivant** *m*, **poursuivante** *f* 1 prosecuting (party) *adj*; 2 plaintiff; prosecutor; pursuer
- partie poursuivante = plaintiff

poursuivre *v* 1 pursue (to); chase (to); 2 prosecute (to)
- être poursuivi pour vol = to be prosecuted for theft
- poursuivre la contrefaçon = to take action for infringement of a patent
- poursuivre quelqu'un au civil = to sue someone
- poursuivre quelqu'un au criminel / au pénal = to prosecute someone
- poursuivre quelqu'un en justice = to prosecute someone; to proceed against someone

pourvoi *m* appeal
- former un porvoi en cassation = to lodge an appeal
- pourvoi en révision = appeal for review

pourvoir (se) *v* **en** appeal to (to)
- se pourvoir en appel = to lodge an appeal

- se pourvoir en cassation = to lodge an appeal (with the Court of Appeal)

pouvoir *m* power; ability; capacity; power of attorney; proxy; authority; discretion
- exercer un pouvoir = to exercise powers of attorney
- législatif pouvoir = legislative power
- munir quelqu'un d'un pouvoir = to furnish someone with full powers
- pouvoir discrétionnaire = discretionary powers
- pouvoir exécutif = executive power
- pouvoir judiciaire = judicial power
- pouvoir par-devant notaire = power of attorney

préalable *adj & m* 1 prior; previous; preliminary; 2 prerequisite; condition; preliminary
- dépôt préalable = advance deposit

préavis *m* prior notice; advance notice (eg to break a contract, discontinue a lease)

précaire *adj & m* 1 precarious *adj*; 2 precarious tenure; precarious holding
- détention d'un bien à titre précaire = precarious holding of a property
- jouir d'un bien par précaire = to enjoy the precarious use of an estate
- location / occupant à titre précaire = precarioue tenancy / occupier
- possession précaire = precarious tenure

précarité *f* precariousness

préciput *m* portion of an estate or inheritance that goes to one of the co-heirs over and above his equal share with the others
- préciput conventionnel = benefit stipulated in the marriage settlement in favour of the surviving spouse

préciser *v* specify (to); state precisely (to); give precise details (to); stipulate (to)
- préciser des régles de procédure = to specify the rules of procedure
- préciser la portée d'un article = to define more accurately the meaning of a clause

préjudice *m* prejudice; tort; wrong; injury
- dommages et intérêts pour préjudice moral = damages for pain and suffering
- porter / faire préjudice à quelqu'un = to inflict injury / loss on someone
- réparer un préjudice = to grant relief for injury
- sans préjudice de mes droits = without prejudice to my rights

prélèvement *m* withdrawal; advance deduction; levy; (commission) charge; standing order (bank); removal *(med)*
- faire / effectuer un prélèvement de sang = to take a blood sample
- ordre de prélèvement = standing order (bank)
- prélèvement d'organes = removal of (body) organs
- prélèvement forfaitaire / libératoire = standard deduction or with-holding tax
- prélèvement sur le capital = capital levy; tax on capital

préméditation *f* premeditation; malice aforethought

preneur *m*, **preneuse** *f* buyer; lessee; leaseholder; tenant; payee (of cheque)

prénommé *m*, **prénommée** *f* above-named; fore-mentioned

prescription *f* prescription; statute of limitations; order; item in contract; specified item; prescription *(med)*
- délai de prescription = period of limitation
- invoquer la prescription = to raise a defence under the statute of limitations
- les prescriptions = regulations; instructions
- les prescriptions techniques = specifications
- loi sur la prescription = statute of limitations
- prescription extinctive = extinctive prescription; time limitation
- prescriptions relatives à la sûreté = safety regulations

prescrire *v* prescribe (to); stipulate (to)
- à la date prescrite = on the prescribed date
- chèque prescrit = out-of-date cheque
- dans le délai prescrit = within the prescribed time
- dans les limites prescrites = within the prescribed limits

prescrit(e) à peine de nullité required by law under penalty of being declared void

présence *f* presence

63

- en présence = face to face (parties, persons)
- les parties en présence = the litigants
présent *adj* present
- le présent contrat = this contract; the present contract
- par le présent (acte, etc) = hereby
présenter (se) *v* appear (to); arise (to); occur (to); present oneself (to)
- se présenter à l'audience = to appear in court
président *m* president; chairman; convener
- Monsieur le président = Your Honour (in court)
présomption *f* presumption; assumption; presumptive evidence; inference
- présomption d'innocence = presumption of innocence
- présomption de fait = presumption of fact
- preuve par présomption = circumstantial evidence; presumptive evidence
prestation *f* 1 prestation (of dues, tolls); 2 provision; lending; loaning (of money); 3 allowance; contribution; benefit(s)
- prestation compensatoire = divorce compensatory settlement
- prestation de serment = taking of an oath; taking the oath
- prestation de service = provision of a service
- prestations en nature = refunding of health care costs; benefits in kind; service charge (paid by tenant to landlord)
- prestation-maladie = sickness benefit
- prestations familiales = family benefits; family allowances (State)
- prestations sociales = national / social insurance benefits
- verser les prestations = to pay out benefits
prêt *m* loan; advance
- prêt à la construction = building loan
- prêt bancaire = bank loan
- prêt relais = bridging loan
prétoire *m* court (floor of)
preuve *f* proof; evidence
- apporter des preuves = to adduce evidence

- commencement de preuve = prima facie evidence; presumptive evidence
- preuve irrecevable = inadmissable evidence
- preuve irréfragable = irrebuttable evidence
- preuve libre = oral evidence admissable
- preuve littérale = documentary evidence
- preuve par présomption = circumstantial evidence; presumptive evidence
- preuve recevable = admissible evidence
prévention *f* 1 prevention; 2 custody; detention; 3 prejudice
- mettre en prévention = to detain; to remand; to take into custody
préventivement *adv* preventively
- arrêter quelqu'un préventivement = to arrest someone on suspicion
- détenu préventivement = committed for trial
- être incarcéré préventivement = to be held or remanded in custody
prévenu,-e *adj*, **prévenu** *m*, **prévenue** *f* 1 charged *adj*; 2 defendant; accused person
- prévenu de vol = charged with theft
prévoir* *v* foresee (to); expect (to); provide for (to)
- la loi prévoit une peine de prison = the law makes provision for a prison sentence
- le code civil prévoit que ... = the civil code provides that ...
- prévu = provided for
prime *f* bonus; premium; subsidy
- prime d'ancienneté = seniority bonus; seniority pay
- prime d'encouragement = incentive bonus
- prime de licenciement = severance pay
- prime de vie chère = cost of living allowance
- prime pour travail de nuit = night work bonus
pris,-e *adj*; **prise** *f* 1 taken; 2 hold; capture
- prise à partie = action against a judge for denial of justice
- prise de contrôle = takeover *(fin)*
- prise de corps = arrest
prison *f* prison

prisonnier *m*, **prisonnière** *f* prisoner
privatif,-ive *adj* depriving of liberty or
rights; exclusive
- avec jardin privatif = with exclusive use
of garden
- droit privatif = exclusive right (of flat,
etc)
- peine privative de liberté = prison
sentence
privation *f* deprivation; deprival
- la privation de la vue / d'un membre =
loss of one's sight / a limb
- la privation des droits civils (ou civiques)
= the deprivation of civil rights
privé,-e *adj* private
- agir en son propre et privé nom = to act
in one's own name
- intérêts privés = private interests
- propriété privée = private property
privilège *m* 1 privilege; 2 preferential right;
preference
- privilège d'hypothèque = mortgage
charge
- privilège de créancier = creditor's
preferential claim
- privilège général = general lien
- avoir un privilège sur quelque chose = to
have a lien / a charge on something
probant,-e *adj* probative; convincing;
conclusive; cogent (proof, evidence,
reason, etc)
- document en forme probante =
document in an authentic form
probation *f* probation
- agent de probation = probation officer
- stage de probation = probationary period
procédure *f* procedure; proceedings
- procédure accusatoire = accusatorial
procedure
- procédure arbitrale = arbitration
proceedings
- procédure civile = civil law procedure
- procédure de conciliation = conciliation
procedure
- procédure de faillite = bankruptcy
proceedings
- procédure de prise en charge = care
proceedings
- procédure en matière familiale =
domestic proceedings

- procédure inquisitoire = inquisitorial
procedure
- procédure pénale = criminal law
procedure
procès *m* (legal) proceedings; (court)
action; lawsuit; trial
- abandonner un procès = to withdraw an
action
- engager un procès contre quelqu'un = to
engage in legal proceedings against
someone
- faire / intenter un procès à quelqu'un =
to start legal proceedings against
someone
- intenter un procès en divorce = to
institute divorce proceedings
- gagner / perdre son procès = to win /
lose one's case
- nouveau procès = new trial
- procés civil = civil proceedings; civil
case
- procès entaché d'un vice de procédure =
mistrial
procès-verbal *m*; **procès-verbaux** *mpl*
1 report or statement (written); 2 record
(eg of evidence); 3 minutes (of a meeting)
- dresser le procès-verbal d'un délit = to
take down the particulars of a minor
offence (by policeman)
- dresser procès-verbal = to draw up a
report; to report
- faire un procès-verbal = to draw up a
report
procuration *f* procuration; proxy; power of
attorney
- avoir procuration sur un compte en
banque = to have power of attorney
over a bank account
- lettre de procuration = power of
attorney; letter of authority
- par procuration = by proxy; per pro
- procuration écrite = authorization in
writing
- procuration générale = full power of
attorney
procureur *m* 1 prosecutor; 2 procurator;
proxy
- procureur de la République = state
prosecutor; Head of the Prosecution at
courts of first instance

- procureur général = public prosecutor
projet *m* project; plan; scheme; rough draft
- établir un projet d'accord / de contrat = to produce a draft agreement / contract
- projet d'acte = draft conveyance document
- projet de loi = draft bill
promesse *f* promise; assurance; undertaking to pay; promissory note *(com)*
- promesse bilatérale = bilateral agreement to sell / buy
- promesse de mariage = promise of marriage
- promesse de vente = unilateral agreement to sell; preliminary contract to sell
- promesse synallagmatique = bilateral agreement to sell / buy
- violation de promesse de mariage = breach of promise
prononcé,-e *adj*; prononcé *m* 1 marked; pronounced; 2 pronouncement
- prononcé du jugement = verdict
prononcer *v* pronounce (to); deliver a verdict (to)
- prononcer sur-le-champ = to adjudicate or pronounce immediately
- prononcer une sentence = to pass / deliver a sentence
- se prononcer sur = to reach a verdict on / about; to come to a decision on / about
prononciation *f* pronouncement
propos *m* 1 purpose; intention; 2 remark
- agir de propos délibéré = to act deliberately
- propos injurieux = abusive words
propre *adj* 1 clean; honest; 2 own (possess)
- biens propres = personal property
propriétaire *m,f* proprietor; proprietess; landlord; landlady; owner; landowner
- nu propriétaire = bare owner
- propriétaire indivis = joint owner
propriété *f* property; proprietorship; ownership; land; estate
- en pleine propriété = as legal owner
- nue propriété = bare ownership; ownership without usufruct
- origine de propriété = vendor's title to property

- pleine propriété (foncière) = freehold
- propriété foncière = property ownership; landed property
- propriété immobilière = real estate
- propriété industrielle = patent rights
- propriété intellectuelle = intellectual property
- propriété libre = property held in fee simple; freehold
- propriété littéraire = literary property
prorogation *f* extension of time; extension of payment period; renewal (of a loan)
- prorogation d'enquête = leave to protract an enquiry
- prorogation d'un prêt = renewal / extension of a loan
- prorogation (légale) du bail = extension of lease (under same conditions)
prostitution *f* prostitution
protéger *v* protect (to); shield (to)
protestation *f* protest; protestation; protesting; affirmation
- faire une protestation de son innocence = to protest one's innocence
protester *v* protest (to); declare (to); affirm (to); profess (to)
protêt *m* protest
provisionnel,-elle *adj* provisional
- accompte provisionnel = payment (of income tax) made on provisional assessment
proxénétisme *m* procuring
- inculpé de proxénétisme = charged with living off immoral earnings
pseudonyme *m* assumed name; alias; pen name; stage name
publiciste *m,f* 1 advertising executive; publicist; 2 public law specialist
publicité *f* advertising; publicity
- la publicité des débats = the public nature of the proceedings
- publicité foncière = land registration; public availability of details of property mortgages
- publicité mensongère = misleading representation
puissance *f* power; strength
- être en puissance de mari = to be under a husband's authority

66

- puissance paternelle = authority of father (mother when father is dead) over child

pupille *m,f* ward
- pupilles de l'État = orphans in state care

purger *v* purge (to); cleanse (to)
- purger un hypothèque = to redeem a mortgage
- purger une peine = to serve a sentence

putatif,-ive *adj* putative; presumed
- mariage putatif = putative marriage
- père putatif = putative father

pyromane *m,f* pyromaniac; arsonist

Q

qualifié,-e *adj* qualified; skilled; aggravated
- vol qualifié = aggravated theft

qualité *f* quality; position
- avoir qualité pour = to have authority to
- en qualité de salarié = as a salaried employee
- qualité substantielle d'un crime = essence of a crime
- qualités d'un jugement = record of proceedings before judgement

quantum *m*, **quanta** *mpl* amount; proportion; ratio
- fixer le quantum des dommages-intérêts = to fix the amount of damages; to assess the damages

quittance *f* receipt; bill; invoice

quote-part *f*; **quotes-parts** *fpl* share; proportional share; quota; portion; contribution pro rata

quotité *f* quota; share
- quotité disponible = disposable portion of estate; share of estate at the free disposal of the testator

R

rachat *m* repurchase; surrender (of insurance policy); redemption (of annuity)

- avec faculté de rachat = with option of repurchase / redemption
- pacte de rachat = covenant of redemption
- rachat d'une servitude = commutation of an easement or right of user
- valeur de rachat = surrender value

racolage *m* soliciting

rang *m* rank; row
- avoir même rang que = to rank equally with (eg debt, mortgage)
- un rang antérieur = an earlier rank; a prior rank

rapport *m* report; (*pl*) relations; relationship
- rapports sexuels = sexual relations

rapt *m* kidnapping; abduction of a minor
- rapt par séduction = abduction with consent

rature *f* erasure
- faire une rature = to cross out; to scratch out; to erase

réassignation *f* resummons; fresh summons; reallocation *(fin)*

réassigner *v* reassign (to); resummon (to); reallocate (to) *(fin)*

recel *m*; **recelé** *m*; **recèlement** *m* receiving and concealing (stolen goods); concealment (of child, part of estate of deceased person); harbouring (of criminal)

receler *v* receive (to) (stolen goods); harbour (to) (criminal); conceal (to)

receleur *m*, **receleuse** *f* receiver (of stolen goods); fence

recevabilité *f* admissibility

recevable *adj* admissible (claim, evidence, etc); allowable; competent (person)
- être recevable dans une demande = to be entitled to proceed with a claim
- témoignage non recevable = inadmissible evidence

rechercher *v* seek (to); hunt for (to); look for (to); research (to)

récidive *f* 1 second offence; subsequent offence; relapse into crime; 2 recurrence (of disease)
- en cas de récidive = in the event of a subsequent offence
- escroquerie avec récidive = second offence of fraud

récidiver *v* 1 reoffend (to); commit a

second offence (to); 2 recur (to) (disease)

récidiviste *m,f* persistant offender; habitual offender

réclusion *f* reclusion; imprisonment
- réclusion criminelle = imprisonment
- réclusion criminelle à perpétuité = life imprisonment

réclusionnaire *m,f* convict

recomparaître *v* appear (in court) again (to)

reconduction *f* renewal (of lease)
- reconduction tacite = renewal (of lease) by tacit agreement

reconnaissance *f* recognition (eg of a right); acknowledgement; gratitude
- donner quelqu'un une reconnaissance (de dette) = to give someone an IOU
- reconnaissance d'un enfant naturel = legitimation; recognition of an illegitimate child
- reconnaissance d'un fait = admission
- reconnaissance d'une responsabilité = admission of liability
- reconnaissance de paternité judiciaire = affiliation order
- reconnaissance du mont-de-piété = pawn ticket

reconnaître *v* recognise (to); recognise legally (to); legitimate (to); acknowledge (to)
- reconnaître la compétence d'un tribunal = to recognise the competence of a court
- reconnaître quelqu'un coupable = to find someone guilty
- reconnaître un fait = to admit

reconstituer *v* reconstruct (to)

recourir *v* run again (to)
- recourir à = to resort to; to have recourse to; to turn to
- recourir à la justice = to take legal proceedings
- recourir contre quelqu'un = to lodge an appeal against someone

recours *m* resort; recourse; appeal; remedy
- avoir un recours sur un chargement = to have a lien upon a cargo
- recours à l'arbitrage = appeal to arbitration
- recours contentieux = submission for a legal settlement

- recours contre des tiers = recourse against third parties
- recours en appréciation de légalité = judicial review
- recours en cassation = appeal to the supreme court
- recours en grâce = plea for pardon; plea for clemency; petition for reprieve
- recours gracieux = submission for an out-of-court settlement
- recours juridique = legal redress; legal remedy
- recours porté devant = appeal brought before / to
- recours pour excés de pouvoir = appeal against ultra vires adminstrative acts
- sans aucun recours = without legal remedy

recouvrement *m* recovery (eg of debt)

rectification *f* rectification; amendment

rectifier *v* rectify (to); amend (to)

reçu *m* receipt

récuser *v* challenge (to) (eg witness); impugn (to) (eg evidence)
- récuser un argument = to make objection to an argument

rédaction* *f* drafting; wording; drawing-up (eg of deed)
- rédaction de bail = drawing-up a lease

rédemption *f* redemption (eg of loan); recovery (eg of right)

redevance *f* rent; rental; rental charge; fee; tax
- redevance emphytéotique = ground rent
- redevance foncière = ground rent
- redevance ordures ménagères = domestic waste (removal) charge
- redevances d'auteur = author's royalties

rédhibitoire *adj* crippling; damning (eg fault)
- vice rédhibitoire = redhibitory defect (eg in horse); latent effect that makes a sale void

rédiger *v* draw up (to); draft (to); write (to); make out (to) (document, lease, agreement, contract, invoice, cheque, etc)
- rediger un contrat = to draw up a contract; to draft a contract

redressement *m* recovery; re-establishment
- maison de redressement = reformatory

- redressement fiscal = tax adjustment
- redressement judiciaire = receivership; administration of a company under judicial supervision
- être mis en redressement judiciaire = to go into receivership

référé *m* summary procedure
- juger en référé = to try a case (sitting) in Chambers
- ordonnance de référé = order delivered by judge sitting in Chambers; provisional order; injunction

réformer *v* 1 reform (to); correct (to); 2 reverse (to) (eg judgement); quash (to)

refus *m* refusal; contempt of court
- refus d'obeissance = insubordination *(mil)*
- refus de comparaître = refusal to appear in court

régime *m* regime; system; scheme
- régime complémentaire = supplementary scheme
- régime de la communauté des biens = marriage agreement under which husband's and wife's property is jointly owned
- régime de la séparation de biens = marriage agreement under which each spouse retains ownership of his / her property
- régime matrimonial = marriage agreement / settlement
- régimes matrimoniaux = rules relating to matrimonial property

registre *m* **(see also Fichier)** register
- les registres de la police = police records
- registre d'état civil = register of births, marriages and deaths
- registre des sociétés = Companies register

règle *f* rule
- agir dans les règles = to act within the rules; to act according to rule
- reçu en règle = formal receipt
- règles contraignantes = constraining rules; restrictive rules
- règles d'exploitation = operating rules
- tout est en règle = everything is in order

règlement *m* 1 regulation(s); 2 settlement; payment (eg of an invoice)

- règlement à l'amiable = out-of-court settlement
- règlement arbitral = settlement by arbitration
- règlement intégral = payment in full
- règlement intérieur = rules and regulations; byelaws
- règlement judiciaire = (compulsory) liquidation
- règlements militaires = army regulations
- règlement par chèque = payment by cheque

réglementation *f* making of rules; regulating; control; regulations; rules
- réglementation des changes = exchange controls
- réglementation en vigueur = regulations in force

régler *v* settle (to) (a bill, a problem)
- non réglé = outstanding, unpaid
- régler des différends = to settle disputes
- régler quelque chose à l'amiable = to settle something out of court
- régler une succession = to settle an estate

relater *v* relate v; recount (to); record (to) (facts)

relation *f* relation; connection
- avoir des relations (sexuelles) avec une femme = to have sexual intercourse with a woman
- relation de causalité = remoteness of damage

reléguer *v* relegate (to)

relevé *m* statement; return
- relevé bancaire = bank statement
- relevé d'identité bancaire = bank account number / details

relever* *v* raise up again (to); lift up again (to)
- les charges relevées contre l'accusé = the charges laid / made against the accused

remboursement *m* repayment; refund; refunding; reimbursement

réméré *m* right of reemption
- vendre à réméré = to sell with a right of reemption

remettre *v* put back (to); replace (to); put off (to); adjourn (to)

remise* *f* delivery; handing over
- remise d'une dette = remission or cancellation of a debt
- remise de parts = transfer of a legacy
- remise des clefs = handing over of keys (eg of flat)

renoncer *v* renounce (to); give up (to); waive (to); withdraw (to)
- renoncer à des poursuites = to abandon a prosecution
- renoncer à toute prétention = to abandon any claim

renonciation *f* renunciation; waiver
- renonciation à un droit = waiver; renunciation of a right
- renonciation à une succession = renunciation of an inheritance

renseignement *m* information; details; particulars
- demande de renseignements = request for information / details

rente *f* income; annuity; pension; rent
- rente foncière = ground rent; land rent
- rente viagère = life annuity; life interest
- rente viagère avec réversion = reversionary annuity; survivorship annuity

renvoi* *m* sending back; return; referral
- demande de renvoi devant une autre juridiction = request for transfer of (court) proceedings
- renvoi = marginal alteration; insertion (in document)

renvoyer* *v* send back (to); return (to); dismiss (to) (eg employee); discharge (to) (eg defendant); postpone (to); put off (to)
- l'affaire sera renvoyée à huitaine = the case will be postponed for a week
- renvoyer le plaideur de sa demande = to nonsuit the plaintiff
- renvoyer le prévenu à une autre audience = to remand the prisoner
- renvoyer une question à une juridiction = to refer a question to a court

réparation *f* redress; remedy; restoring
- accorder réparation = to grant / give redress
- demander réparation de = to seek redress for
- réparation du préjudice = redress for injury or damage

répartition *f* distribution; sharing out; allocation
- mode de répartition du partage des honoraires = way the fees are allocated

répondre *v* answer (to); reply (to)
- répondre à une accusation = to answer a charge

reporter *v* take back (to); postpone (to); defer (to)
- le jugement est reporté à huitaine = the sentence has been deferred for a week

représentation *f* representation; production or exhibition (of documents)
- avoir la représentation exclusive de ... = to be sole agents for ...
- contrat de représentation = agency agreement
- mandataire qui assure la représentation de son mandant = proxy representing his / her principal
- venir par représentation à une succession = to inherit by right of representation

représenter *v* represent (to); present again (to); produce or exhibit documents (to) (eg before a court)
- représenter quelqu'un en justice = to represent someone; to hold a brief for someone

reprise *f* repossession
- procédure de reprise = repossession proceedings

reprocher *v* reproach (to)
- les faits qui lui sont reprochés = the charges against him
- reprocher un témoignage = to take exception to the evidence

répudier *v* repudiate (to); renounce (to); relinquish (to) (eg succession)

requérant *m*; **requérante** *f* applicant

requérir *v* call for (to); require (to); claim (to); demand (to) (eg a penalty)
- la cour requiert que vous comparaissiez = the court requires you to attend
- le procureur est en train de requérir = the prosecutor is making his closing speech; the prosecutor is in course of summing up

requête *f* petition; claim; request
- adresser une requête à un juge = to

70

petition a juge
- requête civile = appeal to a court against a judgement (in case of a gross miscarriage of justice)
- requête en cassation = appeal
- requête en divorce = petition for divorce
- requête en faillite = petition in bakruptcy

réquisition *f* requisition; closing speech (by prosecutor) (also in pl)

réquisitoire *m* closing speech for the prosecution; instruction or brief (to examining magistrate); charge; indictment

rescision *f* recision; annulment; avoidance (of contract, due to mistake or misrepresentation)

réserve *f* reserve; reservation
- signature sans réserve = clean signature
- sous réserve de mes droits = without prejudice to my rights
- sous réserves de = save for
- sous réserve de modification = subject to alteration
- sous réserve que = provided that
- réserve légale / réserve héréditaire = legal share; that part of a legacy which must devolve upon the heirs
- réserve liquide = liquid assets

résidence *f* residence
- résidence principale = main residence
- résidence secondaire = secondary residence; week-end cottage

résiliation *f* termination; cancellation; rescinding; annulment; avoidance (of contract, etc)
- résilation d'un contrat = cancellation of a contract
- résiliation du bail = termination of a lease

résilier *v* annul (to); cancel (to); terminate (to); avoid (to) (eg agreement)
- le preneur a le droit de résilier le bail à tout moment = the tenant has the right to terminate the lease at any time

résoluble *adj* annullable; cancellable; voidable (eg contract)

résolution *f* resolution; solution; cancellation; annulment (eg contract)
- action en résolution = action for recision of contract

- resolution d'un contrat = cancellation of a contract; avoidance of a contract
- resolution du bail = cancellation of the lease

résolutoire *adj* resolutive
- condition résolutoire = resolutive condition; (unfulfilled or unforeseen condition which can ipso facto terminate the contract)

résoudre *v* solve (to); resolve (to); cancel (to); annul (to); rescind (to) (eg contract, sale)

respect *m* respect; regard
- respect du corps humain = respect for the human body

responsabilité *f* liability; responsibility; accountability (finance)
- dénégation de responsabilité = denial or disclaimer of responsibility
- la responsabilité est retenue contre = the defendant is liable
- responsabilité atténuée = diminished responsibility
- responsabilité civile = tortious liability; third party risk
- responsabilité conjointe = joint liability
- responsabilité conjointe et solidaire = joint and several liability
- responsabilité contractuelle = contractual liability
- responsabilité de l'employeur = employer's liability
- responsabilité du fait d'autrui = vicarious liability
- responsabilité indivisible = unseverable responsability
- responsabilité objective = strict liability
- responsabilité pénale = criminal responsibility
- responsabilité pleine et entière = full and entire responsibility
- responsabilité séparée = several liability
- s'exonérer de responsabilité = to avoid liability

responsable *adj* responsible; liable
- être civilement responsable = to be legally responsible
- vous êtes considéré comme responsable = you are held to be liable

ressaisir *v* seize again (to); recover

possession of (to)
- ressaisir un tribunal d'une affaire = to bring a matter before a court again

ressort *m* jurisdiction; competence
- en dernier ressort = in the last resort; in the final jurisdiction (Supreme Court); without appeal
- être du ressort de la cour = to be within the competence of the court

ressortir *v* come under the jurisdiction of (to); be the concern of (to)

restitution *f* restitution
- restitution d'indu = return of payment made in error

résumé *m* summary; summing-up
- résumé d'une affaire pénale = summing-up of a criminal case
- résumé des débats = summing-up

résumer *v* summarize (to); sum up (to)

retenir* *v* hold back (to); retain (to); accept (to) (eg plan, charge)
- l'autre chef d'accusation n'a pas été retenu = the other charge has not been proceeded with
- le jury a retenu la préméditation = the jury accepted the charge of premeditation

rétention *f* retention
- droit de rétention de marchandises = lien on goods
- rétention d'informations = withholding information

retour *m* return; reversion (eg of an inheritance)
- droit de retour = reversion

retourner *v* turn over / up / down / back (to); return (to)
- se retourner contre quelqu'un = to take proceedings against someone; to round on someone

rétractable *adj* revocable

rétracter *v* retract (to); withdraw (to) (eg statement)
- rétracter un arrêt = to retract a decree

retrait *m* withdrawal
- retrait de fonds = withdrawal of capital
- retrait de plainte = nonsuit
- retrait du permis de conduire = suspension of driving licence

retraite *f* 1 retirement (from work);

2 pension
- retraite anticipée = early retirement
- toucher sa retraite = to draw one's pension

rétroactif,-ive *adj* retrospective; retroactive

rétroactivement *adv* retrospectively; retroactively

rétrocéder *v* retrocede (to); cede back (to); reassign (to) (eg right)

rétrocession *f* retrocession; retrocedence; reconveyance

revenu *m* income; revenue
- impôt sur le revenu = income tax
- revenu minimum d'insertion (RMI) = professional society's minimum benefit paid to those with no other source of income
- revenu non salarial = unearned income
- revenu salarial = earned income

réversible *adj* reversible; revertible (eg succession)

réversion *f* reversion
- rente viagère avec réversion = reversionary annuity; survivorship annuity

revêtir *v* put on (to); assume (to); append (to) (eg signature)
- revêtir un document de sa signature = to append one's signature to a document

révocation *f* revocation; cancellation
- révocation du legs = revocation of legacy or part of legacy
- révocation du testament = revocation of will
- révocation expresse = explicit revocation (of an earlier will, etc)
- révocation tacite = tacit revocation (of an earlier will, etc)

révocatoire *adj* revocatory
- acte notarié révocatoire sans forme de testament = revocatory deed to avoid the complicated formalities of an authentic will
- testament révocatoire = revocatory will

révoquer *v* revoke (to); rescind (to)
- révoquer quelque chose en doute = to question (statement, evidence)
- révoquer unilatéralement = to repudiate

risque *m* risk
- cela constitue un risque pour la santé =

that is a health risk / hazard
- police tous risques = comprehensive, all-risks, policy
- risque du recours de tiers = third-party risk
- risque locatif = tenant's third-party risk

rixe *f* affray; brawl

rogatoire *adj* rogatory (commission)

rôle *m* role; part; roll; list; cause list; roll (of court); register

rupture *f* breaking off; breach; rupture
- rupture de contrat = breach of contract
- rupture de promesse de mariage = breach of promise of marriage

S

saisi *m* distrainee; person distrained

saisie *f* seizure (court order); distraint; attachment; execution; foreclosure
- lever la saisie = to withdraw the seizure
- opérer une saisie = to seize
- saisie conservatoire = seizure, by a court, of goods whose ownership is in dispute
- saisie d'une hypothèque = foreclosure of a mortgage
- saisie de biens = seizure of property
- saisie-exécution *f* = distraint (for sale by court order)
- saisie immobilière = seizure of property
- saisie pour loyer = distress
- saisie sur salaire = seizure of pay; seizure of salary

saisie-arrêt *f* attachment; distraint
- décision de saisie-arrêt sur salaire = attachment of earnings order

saisine *f* 1 submission of a case to the court; submission; reference; 2 seisin; legal possession of a freehold estate

saisir *v* submit (to); refer (to); seize (to); distrain (to); take into custody (to)
- la cour a été saisie de l'affaire = the case has been submitted to the court
- saisir la Cour de Justice = to complain to the Court of Justice
- saisir un tribunal d'une affaire = to lay a matter before a court
- saisir une hypothèque = to foreclose a mortgage

saisissable *adj* 1 perceptible; 2 seizable; distrainable; subject to seizure

saisissant,-e *adj*; **saisissant** *m* 1 distraining; 2 distrainer

salaire *m* pay; wages; salary
- échelle mobile des salaires = sliding pay scale
- égalité des salaires = equal pay
- salaire annuel / mensuel = annual / monthly pay or salary
- salaire au forfait = fixed wage; fixed salary
- salaire brut = gross pay
- salaire d'embauche = starting pay or salary
- salaire de base = basic pay or salary
- salaire horaire minimum = minimum hourly wage
- salaire minimum interprofessionnel garanti = guaranteed minimum pay
- salaire net = net pay; take-home pay

salarié *m*, **salariée** *f* wage-earner; salaried employee

sanction *f* sanction; remedy; punishment; penalty

sauf *prep* except; but; save; unless
- sauf accord contraire; sauf convention contraire = unless otherwise agreed
- sauf avis contraire = unless you hear to the contrary
- sauf imprévu = unless anything unforeseen occurs

sauvegarde *f* safeguard; safe keeping
- mise sous la sauvegarde de la justice = placing under the protection of the court

sceau *m*, **sceaux** *mpl* seal, seals

scellé *m* seal (official)
- apposer les scellés = to affix the seals (to prevent unlawful entry)
- bris de scellés = breaking of seals
- faire apposer des scellés sur les biens d'une succession = to have seals placed on the property of an estate
- lever les scellés = to remove the seals
- sous scellés = under seal

securité *f* safety

- securité de l'emploi = security of employment
- securité sociale = social security

selon *prep* in accordance with; pursuant to; under; by virtue of

sentence *f* sentence
- prononcer une sentence = to pass a sentence

séparation *f* separation; splitting
- ordonnance de séparation = judicial separation order
- régime de la séparation de biens = marriage settlement under which husband and wife administer their separate properties
- séparation à l'amiable = voluntary separation
- séparation de corps = legal separation
- séparation de fait = de facto separation; voluntary separation
- séparation des patrimoines = law under which the creditors of the deceased have prior claim on the estate

séparé,-e *adj* separate; separated (eg persons)

séparer *v* divide (to); separate (to) (eg husband and wife); part (to)

séquestration *f* 1 sequestration of goods; 2 isolation of infected animals; 3 seclusion; illegal restraint; false imprisonment

séquestre *m* 1 sequestration (of property); embargo (on ship); confiscation; 2 receiver; depositary; trustee; administrator (of sequestrated property); sequestrator
- compte séquestre = stakeholder account
- en séquestre, sous séquestre = sequestered
- lever le séquestre = to lift the sequestration order
- ordonnance de mise sous séquestre = receiving order (in bankruptcy case)
- séquestre judiciaire = writ of sequestration

serment *m* oath
- affirmer sous serment = to swear on oath
- déclaration sous serment; attestation sous serment = affidavit
- déférer le serment à quelqu'un = to administer the oath to someone; to swear (witness); to swear in (jury)
- faire prêter serment à quelqu'un = to put someone on oath
- faux serment = false oath; perjury
- prestation de serment = taking of an oath; taking the oath
- prêter serment = to take an oath
- sous serment = under oath; on oath

servitude *f* easement; constraint; charge; encumbrance
- immeuble sans servitudes ni hypothèques = estate free from encumbrances
- servitude de passage = right of way
- servitude occulte = undisclosed easement
- servitudes privées grevant le terrain = private easements attached to the land / site

session *f* session; sitting; term (at law courts)

siege *m* seat; head office; bench (magistrates)

signature *f* signing; signature
- apposer sa signature = to append one's signature

signer *v* sign (to)

signification *f* significance; meaning; notification
- signification d'actes = serving of documents

signifier *v* mean (to); signify (to); serve notice of (to); notify (to)
- signifier son congé à quelqu'un = to give someone notice of dismissal
- signifier un acte judiciaire - to serve legal process
- signifier un arrêt à quelqu'un = to serve a notice on someone

simuler *v* feign (to); simulate (to); effect fictitiously (to) (eg sale, contract)
- simuler une maladie = to feign illness; to malinger

sinistre *m* accident; disaster; accidental blaze
- déclarer le sinistre = to notify an accident (for insurance)
- déterminer l'étendu du sinistre = to determine the extent of the damage

sis, sise *adj* located
société *f* 1 society; 2 company; firm; partnership
- société anonyme (SA) = public company; limited company
- société civile = non-trading company
- société à responsabilité limitée (SARL) = private company
soit... soit... conj either... or...; whether... or...
solidaire *adj* 1 joint and several; jointly liable; binding on all parties; 2 interdependent
- obligation solidaire = obligation binding on all parties
- responsabilité (conjointe et) solidaire = joint and several liability
solidairement *adv* jointly
- associés solidairement responsables = jointly liable partners
- conjointement et solidairement = jointly and severally
solidarité *f* 1 joint and several liability; 2 solidarity; 3 interdependence
sommation *f* summons; demand; warning
- faire les sommations d'usage = to give the standard / customary warnings
- recevoir sommation de payer une dette = to receive a demand for payment of a debt
- sommation réitérative = second summons
somme *f* sum; amount (money)
- somme à payer = amount to pay
- somme forfaiture = lump sum
sommer *v* summon (to);
- sommer quelqu'un de / à comparaître = to summon someone to appear
sous-entendu *m* thing understood; implication
sous-seing *m* private agreement; private contract
soussigné *m*, **soussignée** *f*; also *adj* undersigned (the)
- les soussignés déclarent que ... = the undersigned declare that ...
soustraire *v* subtract (to); conceal (to); shield (to)
- soustraire à la compétence de = to exclude from the jurisdiction of

- soustraire quelqu'un aux recherches de la justice = to hide someone from justice
sous-traitant *m* sub-contractor
spécification *f* specification
stipulation *f* stipulation; item in contract; specified item; provision
- stipulation pour autrui = provision for the benefit of a third party
- stipulations d'un contrat = provisions / specifications of a contract
stipuler *v* stipulate (to)
stupéfiant *m* drug; narcotic
subornation *f* bribing; subornation; intimidation (of a witness)
- subornation de témoins = subornation
suborner *v* bribe (to); suborn (to)
subrogation *f* 1 subrogation; substitution; 2 delegation (of powers, rights)
- subrogation à cause de mort = substitution of a deceased party to a contract by another person
- subrogation entre vifs = substitution of one party to a contract by another
subrogé,-e *adj* 1 subrogated; 2 surrogate
- subrogé tuteur = surrogate guardian (appointed by the Family Court)
subroger *v* subrogate (to); substitute (to); appoint as surrogate (to)
subséquemment *adv* subsequently
subséquent,-e *adj* subsequent
substitut *m* deputy public prosecutor
subvention *f* subsidy; subvention; grant
- recevoir une subvention de l'État = to receive a subsidy from the State
succéder à *v* suucceed (to); follow (to); inherit (to); succeed to (to)
succession *f* succession; inheritance; estate
- droits de succession = estate duties; death duties
- la succession est ouverte = the will is undergoing probate
- laisser une succession considérable = to leave a large estate
- partager une succession = to share / divide an estate or inheritance
- succession ab intestat = intestate succession
- succession testamentaire = testate succession

succomber *v* lose a case (to)
suicide *m* suicide
- tentative de suicide = attempted suicide
supposé,-e *adj* estimated; supposed; alleged (eg thief)
surcharge* *f* word(s) written over others (as correction, insertion or over erasure)
surestarie *f* demurrage
- indemnité pour surestaries = demurrage
sûreté *f* safety; reliability; assurance; guarantee
- la Sûreté (nationale) = the (French) criminal investigation department
suroffre *f* higher offer; higher bid
surseoir *v* defer (to); postpone (to); stay (to)
- ordonnance de surseoir = stay of execution
- surseoir à un jugement = to suspend / stay a judgement or proceedings
- surseoir à une inhumation = to postpone a burial
sursis *m* reprieve; suspended sentence
- condamné à six mois de prison avec sursis = given a suspended prison sentence of six months
- peine avec sursis = suspended / deferred sentence
- sursis à exécution / d'exécution = stay of execution
sursitaire *adj* deferred; with a suspended or deferred sentence
surveillance *f* surveillance
survivant,-e *adj*; **survivant** *m*, **survivante** *f* 1 surviving; 2 survivor
susdit,-e *adj* aforesaid; above-mentioned
susmentionné,-e *adj* aforementioned
susnommé,-e *adj*; **susnommé** *m*, **susnommée** *f* above-named; aforenamed; aforementioned
suspect *adj*; **suspect** *m* 1 suspicious; suspect; 2 suspect
suspendre *v* suspend (to); adjourn (to)
suspensif,-ive *adj* suspensive
suspension *f* suspension; stay of proceedings
- arrêt de suspension = injunction
- suspension du permis de conduire = suspension of driving licence; driving ban
syndic *m* trustee; syndic; assignee;

receiver; managing administrator (of a condominium)
- syndic-agréé *m* = official receiver
- syndic de faillite = assignee; official receiver; public trustee (in bankruptcy)
- syndic d'immeuble = managing agent; property manager
syndicat *m* 1 trusteeship (in bankruptcy); 2 syndicate; association; executive committee (of a condominium); 3 trade union
- syndicat de producteurs = producers' association
- syndicat des locataires = tenants' association
- syndicat (ouvrier) = trade union
- syndicat patronal = employers' association or federation
- syndicat professionnel = trade association

T

tacite *adj* tacit; implied
- tacite reconduction = renewal of contract by tacit agreement
tapage *m* din; uproar; racket
- tapage nocturne = disturbance of the peace at night
taux *m* rate; ratio; percentage
- taux d'amortissement = depreciation rate
- taux d'intérêt = interest rate
- taux de crédit minimum = minimum lending rate
- taux de prêt = lending rate
taxe *f* tax; duty (customs); taxation; assessment; surcharge
- taxe à la valeur ajoutée (TVA) = value added tax (VAT)
- taxe d'habitation = community charge; rates
- taxe d'office = arbitrary assessment of income tax
- taxe de publicité foncière = registration / recording tax

- taxe foncière = land tax; property tax
- taxe officielle = tax assessment
- taxe successorale = death duty
- taxe sur la valeur ajoutée = value added tax (VAT)
- taxe sur les spectacles = entertainment tax

taxer *v* tax (to); assess (to)

témoignage *m* testimony; testimonial evidence; witness statement; evidence; hearing (of witnesses)
- d'après son témoignage = according to his statement
- être appelé en témoignage = to be called upon to give evidence
- faux témoignage = false evidence; perjury
- invoquer le témoignage de quelqu'un = to call someone to witness
- reprocher un témoignage = to take exception to the evidence
- témoignage irrecevable / non recevable = inadmissible evidence
- témoignage qui défie toute contradiction = incontrovertible evidence

témoigner *v* testify (to); give evidence (to)
- les faits témoignent en faveur de son dire = the facts corroborate his statement
- témoigner en justice = to testify in court

témoigner de *v* bear witness (to); give evidence (to)

témoin *m* witness
- barre des témoins = witness box
- être témoin à charge / à décharge = to be a witness for the prosecution / for the defence
- être témoin de = to witness; to be a witness of
- témoin à un acte = witness to a signature
- témoin capable = legally competent witness (to a document, will, etc)
- témoin de fait = material witness
- témoin du testament = witness to a will
- témoin instrumentaire = witness to a will or deed; instrumentary witness
- témoin oculaire = eye witness
- suborner un témoin = to bribe / suborn a witness
- venir à la barre des témoins = to take the witness stand

tentative *f* attempt; endeavour
- tentative d'evasion = escape bid / attempt
- tentative de meurtre / de suicide = attempted murder / suicide
- tentative de viol = attempted rape

tenure *f* tenure
- tenure à bail = leasehold

terme *m* term; time; rental period
- arriver à terme = to come to an end (eg plan); to expire (eg contract)
- demander un terme de grâce = to ask for time to pay
- payable à deux termes = payable in two instalments
- payer son loyer à terme échu = to pay one's rent in arrears
- terme de palais = legal term; forensic term

termes *mpl* terms (eg of contract); conditions

terrorisme *m* terrorism

testament *m* will; testament
- absence de testament = intestacy
- caducité du testament = lapsing of a will
- ceci est mon testament = this is my last will and testament
- confection du testament = drawing up of will
- mourir sans testament = to die intestate
- testament antérieur = previous will; earlier will
- testament authentique = will dictated to a notary in the presence of witnesses
- testament de l'interdit judiciaire = will made by legally incompetent person
- testament du mineur = will made by minor (reaching 16 years of age)
- testament international = international will
- testament mystique; testament secret = will written or dictated by testator, signed by him and handed in a sealed envelope, before witnesses, to notary
- testament non instrumenté par notaire = will not drawn up by a notary
- testament notarié; testament devant notaire = will made in the presence of a notary

- testament olographe = will written (in entirety), dated and signed by the testator
- testament ordinaire = usual / ordinary / common (type) will
- testament par acte public; testament authentique = will dictated to notary in the presence of witnesses
- testament postérieur = later will (revoking or complementing an earlier will)
- testament ultérieur = ulterior will; subsequent will
- testament valable = valid will

testateur *m*, **testatrice** *f* testator; one making a will

tester *v* make one's will (to)
- capacité pour tester = legal competency to make a will

tiers *m,inv* third party
- agir pour le compte d'un tiers = to act on behalf of a third party
- tiers bénéficiaire = third party beneficiary

tiers, tierce *adj* third; third party
- l'assurance ne couvre pas les tiers = the insurance doesn't cover third party risks
- tierce caution = contingent liability
- tierce opposition = opposition by third party (in litigation)
- tiers provisionnel = provisional or interim payment of tax
- une tierce personne = a third party

timbré,-e *adj* stamped; bearing a stamp

titre* *m* title; qualification; official document
- au titre de = under (eg an agreement)
- titre de créance = proof of debt
- titre de pension = pension book
- titre exécutoire = enforceable title

titulaire *adj*; **titulaire** *m,f* 1 titular; 2 holder (of right, title, certificate etc); person entitled (eg to right)
- il est déja titulaire de plusieurs condamnations = he already has several convictions recorded against him

tontine *f* tontine
- clause tontine = survivorship clause (on death of a joint owner their share passes to other owner(s))

tort *m* fault; wrong; injury; harm
- avoir tort = to be wrong

tradition *f* 1 tradition; 2 delivery; handing over (of property)

traduire *v* translate (to); express (to);
- traduire quelqu'un en justice = to bring someone before the courts

trafic *m* trafficking; trading; traffic
- faire un trafic = to peddle
- trafic de drogue; trafic de stupéfiants = drug trafficking

transaction *f* transaction; settlement; compromise

transactionnel,-elle *adj* transactional; compromise; settlement
- arriver à une solution transactionnelle = to find a compromise
- formule transactionnelle = compromise formula

transcription *f* transcription; transcribing; registration (of divorce, etc); recording

transiger *v* compromise (to); come to terms (to); come to an agreement (to)
- transiger avec ses créanciers = to come to terms with one's creditors

translation *f* translation; transfer; conveyance (eg right, property)

transport *m* transport; conveyance
- transport d'experts sur les lieux = visit of experts to the scene (of accident, crime etc)

transporter *v* transport (to); convey (to)
- se transporter sur les lieux = to visit the scene (of the accident, crime, etc)

transporteur *m* haulage contractor; carrier; forwarding agent
- transporteur aérien = airline carrier
- transporteur routier = road haulier

travail *m*; **travaux** *mpl* work; occupation;
- certificat de travail = attestation of employment (work record of employee leaving employment)
- conflit du travail = industrial conflict; labour dispute; trade dispute
- contrat de travail = contract of employment
- la durée du travail = working time; work hours per week
- le travail précaire = casual work
- travail à temps complet = full-time job

- travail à temps partiel = part-time job; part-time work
- travail au noir = moonlighting
- travail d'intérêt général = community service
- travail de nuit = night work
- travail posté = shiftwork
- travail temporaire = temporary work
- travaux agricoles = agricultural work
- travaux ménagers = housework
- travaux préparatoires = preliminary documents

travailleur *m*, **travailleuse** *f* worker
- travailleur en bâtiment = building worker
- travailleur handicapé = disabled worker; handicapped worker
- travailleur indépendant = self-employed worker
- travailleur manuel = manual worker

trésor *m* treasure; treasury; treasure trove
- le Trésor public = (local) public revenues department

tribunal *m* court
- incompétence d'un tribunal = lack of jurisdiction
- opposition admise par le tribunal = objection sustained by the court
- tribunal arbitral = court of arbitration
- tribunal correctionnel = court trying cases of a fairly serious nature
- tribunal d'exception = emergency court; special court
- tribunal d'instance = magistrates court; court of first instance (presided over by one judge)
- tribunal de commerce = commercial court
- tribunal de grande instance = higher level court (presided over by three judges)
- tribunal de police = police court (dealing with petty offences attracting a fine)
- tribunal des pensions militaires = military pensions tribunal
- tribunal pour enfants = juvenile court

triennat *m* three-year period
tromperie *f* fraud; deception; cheating
- tromperie sur la marchandise = fraud relating to goods

trouble *m* confusion; disorder; trouble; disturbance
- trouble de jouissance = disturbance of possession; prevention of enjoyment of possession

tutélaire *adj* tutelary; guardian
- gestion tutelaire = guardianship

tutelle *f* guardianship; wardship; protection; tutelage
- enfant en tutelle = child under guardianship
- juge des tutelles = judge administering the property of those persons under guardianship
- sous tutelle = in ward; under the care of

tuteur *m*, **tutrice** *f* guardian
- subrogé tuteur = surrogate guardian (appointed by the Family Court)
- tuteur légal / testamentaire = legal / testamentary guardian

U

unilatéral,-e *adj* unilateral
urbanisme *m* town planning
- certificat d'urbanisme = certificate showing planning status
- disposition d'urbanisme = planning provision; planning requirement

usage *m* use; using; employment
- clause de usage = customary clause
- droit de usage = customary right
- droit de usage continu = right of user

usufruit *m* usufruct; the right to use and enjoy the benefits of another's property; life interest
- avoir / garder l'usufruit de quelque chose = to have / retain the usufruct of something
- plein usufruit de quelque chose = full right of user of something
- quasi-usufruit = quasi usufruct; imperfect usufruct

usufruitier,-ière *adj* usufructuary
usufruitier *m*, **usufruitière** *f* tenant for life; beneficial occupant
usurpation *f* usurpation; unauthorised

vice

assumption (of a right, qualification etc)
usurpatoire *adj* usurpatory
- signature usurpatoire = unauthorized
  signature
usurper *v* usurp (to)
- usurper sur les droits de quelqu'un = to
  encroach or usurp someone's rights
- usurper sur ses voisins = to usurp one's
  neighbours

V

vacant,-e *adj* vacant; unoccupied (eg
house); in abeyance (eg inheritance)
- succession vacante = estate in
  abeyance; estate without a claimant
vacation *f* 1 session; sitting (of officials);
2 *pl* vacation; recess (of law courts);
3 *pl* fees (of lawyers, etc); 4 abeyance (of
succession, rights, etc)
vagabondage *m* vagrancy
vaine pâture *f* common grazing land
valable *adj* valid; legitimate
- effets valables = personal estate of
  some value
- interlocuteur valable = authorized
  representative
valeur *f* value; validity
- valeur actuelle = current value
- valeur indicative = for information only
- valeur légale = legal validity
- valeur locative = rental value
- valeur obligatoire = binding authority
- valeur patrimoniale = patrimonial value
- valeur vénale = market / sale value
- valeurs fiduciaires = paper securities
valide *adj* valid
- non valide = invalid
validement *adv* validly
validité *f* validity
- établir la validité d'un testament = to
  prove a will
vendeur *m*, **vendeuse** *f*; **venderesse** *f*
1 vendor; seller; 2 shop assistant
vente *f* sale
- promesse de vente = preliminary sale

agreement
- vente à l'amiable = sale by private
  treaty
- vente aux enchères = sale by auction
- vente d'un fonds de commerce = sale of
  a business
- vente en l'état futur d'achèvement en
  plan = sale "on plan"
- vente en viager = sale (of property) for a
  life annuity
- vente par adjudication = sale by auction
  of legally seized property
ventilation *f* 1 ventilation; 2 separate
valuation (of chattels or parts of an estate)
ventiler *v* 1 ventilate (to); 2 value
separately (to) (chattels or parts of an
estate)
verdict *m* verdict
- annuler un verdict = to set aside a
  verdict
- prononcer / rendre un verdict = to return
  a verdict
- verdict d'acquittement = verdict of not
  guilty
- verdict de culpabilité = verdict of guilty
vérité *f* truth
vertu *f* virtue
- agir en vertu d'une délégation = to act
  on someone's authority
- en vertu de = by virtue of; under; in
  pursuance of
- en vertu de cet arrangement = under
  this agreement
veuf *m*, **veuve** *f* widowed man, widower;
widowed woman, widow
viager,-ère *adj*; **viager** *m* 1 life interest; for
life; 2 life annuity
- achat en viager = purchase made
  against a life annuity
- mettre / acheter un bien en viager = to
  sell or buy a property in return for a life
  annuity
- rente viagère = life annuity; life interest
vice *m* 1 vice; corruption; 2 flaw; fault;
defect
- entaché d'un vice = vitiated
- vice caché = latent or hidden fault /
  defect
- vice de construction = construction fault
  or defect (building)

- vice de forme = legal flaw; flaw (of a deed, etc); faulty drafting (of a deed, etc)
- vice du consentement = defect of consent
- vice rédhibitoire = redhibitory defect (in horse, etc); latent defect that makes sale void

vicier *v* 1 pollute (to); 2 vitiate (to); invalidate (to) (eg deed, contract)

victime *f* victim; casualty; aggrieved party
- être victime d'un escroc = to be victim of a swindler

viduité *f* widowhood (woman); widower-hood (man); viduity
- délai de viduité = minimum legal period of widowhood / widowerhood

vie *f* life
- vie active = working life
- vie privée = privacy; private life

vif *m* living person
- disposition / donation entre vifs = donation inter vivos

vigueur *f* vigour; strength
- date d'entrée en vigueur = effective date; date of coming into force
- en vigueur = in force

vindicte *f* prosecution (of crime); condemnation
- vindicte publique = prosecution and conviction

viol *m* rape
- tentative de viol = attempted rape

violation *f* violation; breach; desecration
- violation de clôture = breach of close
- violation de domicile = illegal entry / forcible entry (of home)
- violation de la liberté individuelle = infringement of individual freedom
- violation de la loi = breach of law
- violation de promesse de mariage = breach of promise
- violation de sépulture = desecration of a grave

violence *f* violence; act of violence; duress
- actes de violence caractérisés = aggravated assault
- violence armée = armed violence
- violence verbale = verbal abuse
- vol avec violences = robbery with violence

viser *v* initial (to) (document); countersign (to)

visite *f* visiting; visit
- droit de visite aux enfants = right of access to the children
- visite de douane = customs inspection
- visite des lieux = search of the premises
- visite domiciliare = house search
- visites à domicile = doctor's visits

voie *f* way; road;
- voie d'accès = access road
- voie d'action = through a lawsuit
- voie d'appel = lodging of an appeal
- voie de fait = administrative act which is grossly illegal
- voie de fait = assault and battery; infringement of civil liberties
- voie de fait simple = common assault
- voie de raccordement = slip road
- voie de recours = path for appeal
- voie de réquisition = by way of brief (to the court)

voiturier *m* carrier; carter

vol *m* theft
- vol à l'arraché = bagsnatching
- vol à l'étalage = shoplifting
- vol à la roulotte = car theft; theft of objects from cars
- vol à la tire = pickpocketing
- vol à main armée = armed robbery
- vol avec agression = robbery with violence
- vol avec effraction = burglary; robbery with breaking and entering
- vol avec porte d'arme = aggravated burglary
- vol avec violences = robbery with violence
- vol de voiture = car theft
- vol domestique = in-house theft (by an employee)
- vol qualifié = aggravated / compound theft
- vol simple = common theft
- vol tentative = attempted theft

volontairement *adv* voluntarily

volonté *f* desire; willingness; will; animus testandi
- les dernières volontés = last will and testament

- volonté de tester = desire / willingness to make a will
- volonté du testateur = desire / willingness of a testator (to draw up or revoke a will)

vu *m* sight; inspection
- le vu d'un arrêt = the preamble of a decree

ENGLISH-FRENCH
(‡ see French section for examples of usage)

A

abandon (to) abandonner *v*; délaisser‡ *v*
abandonment (eg property, children)
abandon‡ *m*; délaissement‡ *m*
abduction déplacement *m*; enlèvement‡ *m*
abduction of a minor rapt‡ *m*
abeyance (of succession, rights, etc)
vacation *f*
ability capacité‡ *f*; pouvoir‡ *m*; habilité‡ *f*
able idoine‡ *adj*
abortion avortement *m*
about a week une huitaine‡ *f*
above-mentioned susdit,-e *adj*
above-named susnommé,-e *adj*; susnommé
m, susnommée *f*; prénommé *m*,
prénommée *f*
absence absence *f*; défaut *m*
absent-mindedness distraction *f*
absentee absent *m*, absente *f* (also *adj*)
absolution absolution *f*
abstraction distraction *f*
abuse abus‡ *m*; injure‡ *f*
abuse of authority forfaiture *f*
accept (to) (eg plan, charge) accepter *v*;
retenir‡ *v*
acceptance; accepting acceptation‡ *f*
accident accident‡ *m*; sinistre‡ *m*
accommodation unit local‡ *m*, locaux‡ *mpl*
accomplice coauteur *m*; complice *m,f*
account (eg bank) compte‡ *m*
account (exposition) exposé‡ *m*
accountability (finance) responsabilité‡ *f*
accountant comptable *m,f*
**accretion (eg of legacy, of survivors' rights
by death of co-legatee)** accroissement *m*
accumulate (to) cumuler‡ *v*
accumulation (of offences, penalties)
cumul‡ *m*
accusation accusation‡ *f*
accusatory (procedure) accusatoire *adj*
accuse of (to) accuser *v*
accused (the) accusé *m*, accusée *f*;
l'inculpé *m*, l'inculpée *f*
achievement exploit *m*
acknowledge (to) reconnaître‡ *v*

acknowledge (receipt of) (to) accuser *v*
acknowledgement reconnaissance‡ *f*
acquit (to) acquitter *v*
acquittal acquittement *m*; absolution *f*
act of aggression agression *f*
act of violence violence‡ *f*
action (at law) action‡ *f*; procès‡ *m*;
cause‡ *f*; poursuite *f*
address to the court plaidoirie *f*
adjourn (to) ajourner *v*; suspendre *v*
adjournment ajournement *m*
adjudicator arbitre *m*
adjudicate (to) juger *v*
administer administrer *v*
administrative order or decree arrêté‡ *m*
administrator administrateur *m*
administrator (of sequestrated property)
séquestre *m*
admissibility recevabilité *f*
admissible (claim, evidence, etc)
recevable‡ *adj*
admission aveu *m*; déclaration *f*;
reconaissance‡ *f*
admit (to) reconnaître *v*; admettre *v*;
avouer *v*
adopted; adoptive adoptif,-ive‡ *adj*
adoption adoption *f*
adulterine adultérin,-e *adj*
adultery adultère‡ *m*
advance deduction prélèvement‡ *m*
advantage avantage *m*
advertising executive; publicist
publiciste *m,f*
advertising publicité‡ *f*
advice avis *m*; conseil *m*
advocate; barrister avocat‡ *m*; avocate *f*;
défenseur *m*
affect (to); have an effect on (to) affecter *v*
affidavit attestation *f*
affirm (to) confirmer‡ *v*; déposer *v* sans
prêter serment
affirmation protestation‡ *f*
affix (to) (eg seal, signature, stamp)
apposer‡ *v*
affray rixe *f*
aforementioned susmentionné,-e *adj*;
susnommé,-e *adj*; susnommé *m*,

susnommée *f*

aforenamed susnommé,-e *adj*; susnommé *m*, susnommée *f*

aforesaid susdit,-e *adj*

after due hearing of the parties (eg of judgement) contradictoire *adj*

against the regulations indu[‡] *adj*

agent dépositaire[‡] *m,f*

aggravated qualifié,-e[‡] *adj*; aggravé,-e *adj*

aggravation aggravation *f*

aggrieved party victime[‡] *f*

agree (to) convenir *v*; être *v* d'accord

agree (which); which are in agreement concordant,-e *adj*

agreement accord[‡] *m*; arrangement *m*; contrat[‡] *m*; convention[‡] *f*; engagement[‡] *m*; entente[‡] *f*

aid aide[‡] *f*

aiding and abetting complicité *f*

alias pseudonyme *m*

alibi alibi[‡] *m*

alienability mutabilité *f*

alienable mutable *adj*

alienate (to); estrange (to) aliéner *v*

alienation; transfer (of rights, property, etc) aliénation[‡] *f*

alimony pension[‡] *f*; aliments *mpl*

allegation allégation *f*; dire[‡] *m*

alleged (eg thief) supposé,-e *adj*

alleviation atténuation *f*

allocate (to); assign (to) affecter *v*

allocation allocation[‡] *f*; répartition[‡] *f*

allocation (of a building, etc) affectation *f*

allotment; building plot lotissement[‡] *m*

allowable recevable[‡] *adj*

allowance pension[‡] *f*; prestation[‡] *f*; indemnité[‡] *f*

amend (to) rectifier *v*

amendment avenant *m*; rectification *f*

amenities agrément *m*

amicable amiable[‡] *adj*

amount (money) somme[‡] *f*

amount quantum[‡] *m*, quanta[‡] *mpl*

animus testandi volonté[‡] *f*

annexe; extension (to a building) annexe *f*

annuity rente *f*

annul (to) annuler *v*; casser *v*; infirmer *v*; résilier[‡] *v*

annullable; cancellable (eg contract) résoluble *adj*

annulment annulation[‡] *f*; infirmation *f*; rescision *f*; cassation *f*; résiliation[‡] *f*; résolution[‡] *f*

answer (to) répondre[‡] *v*

antichresis antichrèse *f*

apartment; lodging logement *m*

apology apologie *f*

appeal appel[‡] *m*; pourvoi[‡] *m*; recours[‡] *m*

appeal at law appel[‡] *m*

appeal to (to) se pourvoir *v* en

appear (to) se présenter[‡] *v*

appear again (in court) (to) recomparaître *v*

appear before a court of justice (to) comparaître[‡] *v*; ester *v* en justice

appearance (before the court) comparution[‡] *f*

appellant appelant *m*, appelante *f*

appellation appellation[‡] *f*

appellee intimé *m*, intimée *f*

append (to) (signature) apposer *v*; revêtir[‡] *v*

appendix; annexe; supplement (to a document) annexe *f*

applicant impétrant *m*, impétrante *f*; requérant *m*, requérante *f*

application application *f*; demande[‡] *f*

apply for (to) (eg job) postuler *v*; demander *v*

appoint (to) constituer[‡] *v*; nommer *v*; commettre[‡] *v*

appoint (to) (heir, official, etc) instituer[‡] *v*

appoint as surrogate (to) subroger *v*

appointing constitution[‡] *f*

appointing (of heir) institution *f*

appointing a penalty for non-compliance comminatoire *adj*

appraisal; assessment bilan[‡] *m*

apprentice apprenti *m*, apprentie *f*

apprenticeship apprentissage *m*

appropriate idoine[‡] *adj*

appropriation appropriation *f*

approval agrément *m*

approve (to) homologuer *v*

apt apte *adj*

aptitude aptitude *f*

arbitral arbitral,-e *adj*

arbitration arbitrage *m*

arbitrator; arbiter arbitre *m*; conciliateur *m,f*

argument argument *m*

arise (to); occur (to) se présenter[‡] *v*

arrange (to) ordonner *v*

arrangement arrangement *m*; compromis[‡] *m*
arrears; monthly instalments arrérages *mpl*
arrest arrestation[‡] *f*; arrêt *m*
arrest (to); seize (to) arrêter *v*
arson incendie *m* volontaire; incendie *m* criminel
arsonist incendiaire *m,f*; pyromane *m,f*
article article *m*
articled clerk apprenti *m*, apprentie *f*
ascendant ascendant,-e *adj*; ascendant *m*, ascendante *f*
ask for (to); request (to) demander *v*
assail (to) attaquer *v*
assassination assassinat *m*
assassination attempt (political) attentat[‡] *m*
assault and battery coups *mpl* et blessures *fpl*
assent agrément *m*
assertion dire[‡] *m*
assess (to) taxer *v*
asset(s) biens[‡] *mpl*; capital *m*; avoir *m*; actif *m*
assign (to) assigner *v*; céder *v*; déléguer *v*
assign ayant-cause *m*; ayant-droit *m*
assignability (eg of estate) cessibilité *f*
assignable cessible *adj*
assignee cessionnaire *m*; mandataire[‡] *m,f*; syndic[‡] *m*; ayant-droit *m*
assignment cession *f*
assignor cédant *m*, cédante *f*
assistance aide f
associate; partner associé *m*, associée *f*
association association *f*; syndicat[‡] *m*
assume (to) revêtir *v*
assumed name pseudonyme *m*
assumption immixtion[‡] *f*; présomption[‡] *f*
assurance assurance *f*; promesse[‡] *f*; sûreté *f*
assure (to) assurer *v*
attached ci-joint *adj*
attachment saisie[‡] *f*; saisie-arrêt[‡] *f*
attack agression *f*; **attack on (a building)** attentat *m*
attack (to) attaquer *v*
attempt tentative[‡] *f*
attenuated atténué,-e *adj*
attest (to); certify (to) attester *v*; certifier[‡] *v*
attestation attestation[‡] *f*; certification *f*

attract (to) entrainer[‡] *v*
audience; hearing audience *f*
audition audition *f*
authentication certification *f*
authority autorité[‡] *f*; instance[‡] *f*; droit[‡] *m*; pourvoir[‡] *m*
authorization autorisation *f*; habilitation[‡] *f*
authorize (to) autoriser *v*; habiliter[‡] *v*
authorized agent or representative mandataire[‡] *m,f*; fondé[‡] *m* de pouvoir
autopsy autopsie *f*
availability disponibilité *f*
available disponible[‡] *adj*
avoid (to) (eg contract) annuler *v*; résilier[‡] *v*
avoidance (of contract, etc) annulation *f*; résiliation[‡] *f*
avoidance (of contract, due to mistake or misrepresentation) rescision *f*
avowant déclarant *m*, déclarante *f*
award (civil case) jugement[‡] *m*
award (to); bestow (to) décerner *v*

B

back (to) avaliser *v*
bad debt non-valeur *f*
bail bond; surety caution[‡] *f*
bailee dépositaire[‡] *m,f*
bailiff huissier[‡] *m*
bailment (of goods) dépôt *m*
bailor déposant *m*, déposante *f*
balance sheet bilan[‡] *m*
bankruptcy faillite[‡] *f*; déconfiture *f*
banning of; ban on interdiction[‡] *f*
bar barre *f*; barreau *m*
bare owner nu-propriétaire *m*, nue-propriétaire *f*
bargain marché[‡] *m*
bargaining marchandage *m*
barring forclusion *f*
barrister avocat[‡] *m*; avocate *f*
be injurious to (to) nuire[‡] *v*
be payable (to) échoir *v*
be reached (to) (eg agreement) intervenir[‡] *v*
be the concern of (to) ressortir *v*
bear witness (to) attester *v*; témoigner de *v*

bearing a stamp timbré,-e *adj*
become out-of-date (to); expire (to) (eg passport) périmer‡ *v*
becoming a third party in a contract, etc intervention‡ *f*
bed lit‡ *m*
before par-devant‡ *prep & adv*; par-devers *prep*
beginning commencement *m*
below the age of puberty impubère *adj & m,f*
below ci-après *adv*
bench (magistrates) siege *m*
beneficial occupant usufruitier *m*, usufruitière *f*
beneficiary bénéficiaire *m,f*; ayant-droit *m*; ayants-droit *mpl*
beneficiary of a trust fidéicommissaire *m*
benefit from (to) bénéficier *v*
benefit(s) allocation‡ *f*; avantage‡ *m*; bénéfice‡ *m*; indemnité‡ *f*; prestation‡ *f*
bequeath (to) léguer *v*
bequest legs‡ *m*
bias distorsion *f*
bidder offrant‡ *m*
bigamy bigamie *f*
bill quittance *f*; facture *f*
bind (to) lier *v*; obliger *v*; engager‡ *v*
birth; nationality origine‡ *f*
blackmail chantage *m*
blow coup *m*
body corps‡ *m*
body (of dead person); corpse cadavre *m*
bond certificat *m*
bond; link; tie lien *m*
bonus gratification *f*; prime‡ *f*
borrowing emprunt‡ *m*
bottom fond‡ *m*
brawl rixe *f*
breach atteinte‡ *f*; contravention‡ *f*; rupture‡ *f*; violation‡ *f*; manquement‡ *m*
breach of contract inexécution *f*
break (to) casser *v*
breaking bris‡ *m*
breaking and entering cambriolage *m*; effraction‡ *f*
breaking off rupture‡ *f*
breaking-in effraction‡ *f*
breath test alcootest *m*

Breathalyzer™ alcootest *m*
bribe (to) corrompre‡ *v*; suborner *v*
bribery corruption‡ *f*
bribing subornation‡ *f*
bring (to) (an action) actionner *v*; intenter‡ *v* (une action, un procès à, contre quelqu'un)
bring (to) (case to court) déférer‡ *v*
brother(s) and sister(s); collateral; relatives collatéral *m*, collatéraux *mpl*
builder entrepreneur *m*, entrepreneuse *f*
building bâtiment *m*; construction‡ *f*; immeuble‡ *m*; local‡ *m*
building plot lotissement *m*; parcelle *f* de terre
burden (to); encumber (to) (building) grever‡ *v*
burden of proof charge *f* de la preuve
burglary; burgling cambriolage *m*
business entreprise‡ *f*; affaire *f*
business premises immeuble *m*; local‡ *m* commercial
buyer acheteur *m*, acheteuse *f*; acquéreur *m*, acquéreuse *f*; preneur *m*, preneuse *f*
by accumulation cumulativement *adv*

C

cadastral register; cadstral survey cadastre *m*
call (to) appeler *v*
call for (to) requérir‡ *v*
call upon (to) (witness) invoquer‡ *v*
calumny calomnie *f*
cancel (to) annuler *v*; résilier‡ *v*; résoudre *v*
cancellation résiliation‡ *f*; résolution‡ *f*; révocation‡ *f*; anéantissement *m*
capable capable *adj*; compétent,-e *adj*
capacitate (to) habiliter‡ *v*
capacitation habilitation‡ *f*
capacity capacité‡ *f*; pourvoir‡ *m*
capital capital *m*
captation captation *f*
carelessness négligence‡ *f*; imprudence‡ *f*
carrier transporteur‡ *m*; voiturier *m*
carry (to) (eg penalty) entraîner‡ *v*
carry out (to) (eg contract) exécuter *v*

case affaire[‡] *f;* argument *m;* cas[‡] *m;* cause[‡] *f;* dossier[‡] *m*
case law jurisprudence *f*
cashier (to); demote (to) casser *v (mil)*
cassation cassation *f*
casualty victime[‡] *f*
cause; ground cause[‡] *f*
cease (to) cesser[‡] *v*
cede back (to) rétrocéder *v*
cell cellule *f*
censor (to) censurer *v*
censorship censure *f*
censure (to) censurer *v*
censure; reprimand censure *f*
Central Register for the filing of wills
Fichier Central des dispositions de dernières volontés (France)
certificate acte[‡] *m;* certificat *m*
certified report constat[‡] *m*
certified statement constatation *f*
certify (to) attester *v;* certifier[‡] *v*
certify (to) (eg a death) constater *v*
cessionary; endorser (of cheque) cessionnaire *m*
chairman président[‡] *m*
challenge (to) (eg witness) récuser[‡] *v*
changeable; mutable mutable *adj*
character reference certificat *m* de bonne vie et mœurs
charge (to) charger[‡] *v;* inculper *v*
charge accusation *f;* charge *f;* commission *f;* inculpation[‡] *f;* réquisitoire *m*
charge with (to); indict for (to) accuser *v*
charged *adj* prévenu,-e[‡] *adj*
cheating tromperie[‡] *f*
chicanery; pettifoggery chicane *f*
chief chef[‡] *m*
child enfant[‡] *m*
child born of adultery adultérin,-e *adj*
circulate (to); broadcast (to) diffuser *v*
circumstance circonstance *f;* cas *m*
circumstantial (evidence) indirect,-e *adj*
citation; quotation citation *f*
cite (to) citer *v;* invoquer[‡] *v*
civil civil,-e *adj*
civil servant fonctionnaire *m,f*
civilian civil *m*
civilly civilement[‡] *adv*
claim demande[‡] *f;* requête[‡] *f;* droit[‡] *m*
claim *(fin)* créance[‡] *f*

claim (plaintiff's) placet *m*
claim (to) demander *v;* réclamer *v;* revendiquer *v*
clarification éclaircissement[‡] *m*
clash conflit[‡] *m*
clause article *m;* clause[‡] *f;* convention *f;* disposition[‡] *f*
clause; (restrictive) clause modalité[‡] *f*
clean propre *adj*
cleanse (to) purger[‡] *v*
clear explicite *adj;* franc[‡], franche[‡] *adj*
clear (to) innocenter[‡] *v*
clearing up éclaircissement[‡] *m*
clemency grâce[‡] *f*
clerk of the court greffier *m,* greffière *f*
clever; skilful habile *adj*
close fin[‡] *f*
closed hearing huis[‡] *m* clos
closing speech (by prosecutor) réquisition *f;* réquisitoire *m*
clue; piece of evidence indice *m*
co-defendant codéfendeur *m*
co-director coadministrateur *m,* coadministratrice *f*
co-heir(ess) (to be) copartager *v* (une succession)
co-obligant; co-obligor coobligé *m;* coobligée *f*
co-ownership; joint ownership copropriété[‡] *f*
co-respondant codéfendeur *m;* complice[‡] *m,f*
co-trustee coadministrateur *m,* coadministratrice *f*
code code[‡] *m*
codicil codicille *m*
codicillary codicillaire *adj*
codify (to) (laws, etc) codifier *v*
coercion coaction *f;* contrainte[‡] *f*
cogent (proof, evidence, reason) probant,-e *adj*
cohabit (to) cohabiter *v*
cohabitant; co-habitee concubin *m,* concubine *f*
cohabitation cohabitation *f;* concubinage *m*
collaborative commun,-e *adj*
collaborator; co-author coauteur *m*
collect (to) (tax) percevoir *v*
combination of offences concours *m* d'infractions

come to an agreement (to) transiger *v*
come to terms (to) transiger *v*
come under the jurisdiction of (to)
  ressortir *v*
come up (to) passer[‡] *v*
command commandement *m*
commencement commencement *m*
comminatory (decree) comminatoire *adj*
commission commission[‡] *f*
commission charge prélèvement[‡] *m*
commissioner commissaire[‡] *m*
commit (to) (crime, etc) commettre *v*
commit a second offence (to) récidiver *v*
common commun,-e[‡] *adj*
common grazing land vaine pâture *f*
common law husband / wife concubin *m*,
  concubine *f*
common ownership (eg of a wall, fence)
  mitoyenneté *f*
common-law couple concubinage[‡] *m*
common-law marriage concubinage[‡] *m*
commonalty communauté[‡] *f*
community communauté[‡] *f*
commutative (eg contract)
  commutatif,-ive *adj*
company benefit scheme œuvres *fpl*
  sociales
company; firm; partnership société[‡] *f*
compel (to); force (to) contraindre[‡] *v*;
  obliger *v*
compensate (to) compenser *v*;
  dédommager *v*; indemniser[‡] *v*
compensation dédommagement[‡] *m*;
  indemnité[‡] *f*; compensation[‡] *f*;
  contrepartie[‡] *f*
competence; competency compétence[‡] *f*;
  habilité[‡] *f*; ressort[‡] *m*
competent recevable[‡] *adj*; compétent,-e[‡]
  adj; habile *adj*
compilation (of inventory) confection *f*
complain (to) se plaindre[‡] *v*
complainant demandeur[‡] *m*,
  demanderesse[‡] *f*
complaint plainte[‡] *f*
complicity complicité *f*
comply (to) conformer[‡] *v*
compromise transactionnel,-elle[‡] *adj*
compromise compromis *m*
compromise (to) transiger *v*
compulsion coaction *f*; contrainte[‡] *f*

compulsory purchase of private property
  expropriation *f*
compulsory surrender of real estate
  expropriation *f*
computer ordinateur *m*; informatique[‡] *adj*
computer science; computing
  informatique[‡] *f*
conceal (to) cacher *v*; dissimuler *v*; receler
  v; soustraire[‡] *v*
concealment dissimulation[‡] *f*; recel *m*
concealment (eg of child, part of estate of
  deceased person) recel *m*; recelé *m*;
  recèlement *m*
concern (to) concerner *v*
concession concession *f*; octroi[‡] *m*
conciliate (to) concilier *v*
conciliation conciliation *f*
conciliatory conciliatoire *adj*
conclude (to) conclure[‡] *v*
conclusion conclusion[‡] *f*
conclusive; convincing (proof, etc)
  probant,-e *adj*
condemnation vindicte[‡] *f*
condition état[‡] *m*
condition; requirement; condition[‡] *f*
conditions termes *mpl*
conduct a survey (to) enquêter[‡] *v*
confession aveu[‡] *m*
confirm (to) confirmer[‡] *v*; homologuer *v*
confiscate (to) confisquer *v*
confiscation confiscation *f*; séquestre[‡] *m*
conflict conflit[‡] *m*
conform (to) conformer[‡] *v*
confusion confusion[‡] *f*; trouble[‡] *m*
connection relation[‡] *f*
consanguinity in direct line filiation[‡] *f*
consecutive consécutif,-ive *adj*
consensual (eg contract)
  consensuel,-elle *adj*
consent aveu[‡] *m*; consentement[‡] *m*;
  agrément *m*
consent (to) accepter *v*
consenting; willing consentant,-e *adj*
consequential consécutif,-ive *adj*
consider (to) considérer[‡] *v*
considered censé *adj*
consignee consignataire *m*
consignment consignation *f*; envoi *m*;
  expédition *f*
conspiracy complot *m*

conspire (to) comploter v
constituent constituant m
constitute (to) constituer[‡] v
constitution constitution f
constrain (to) contraindre[‡] v
constraint astreinte f; contrainte[‡] f;
servitude[‡] f
construction; building construction[‡] f
contempt of court outrage m à magistrat;
refus[‡] m
content; substance fond[‡] m
contentious adj contentieux,-ieuse adj
contest (to) (eg inheritance, right,
competence) contester v
contest (to) (judgement, testimony)
attaquer v
contestation contestation[‡] f
contract contrat[‡] m
contract; lump-sum contract forfait[‡] m
contracting adj contractant,-e adj
contracting party contractant m,
contractante f
contractor entrepreneur m, entrepreneuse f
contractual (eg deed, clause)
conventionnel,-elle[‡] adj; contractuel,-elle
adj
contradiction contradiction[‡] f
contradictory; conflicting contradictoire adj
contravene (to) contrevenir v
contribute (to) cotiser v
contribution pro rata quote-part f; quotes-
parts fpl
contribution apport[‡] m; cotisation[‡] f;
contribution f
contributive contributif,-ive adj
contributor intervenant m, intervenante f
contributory contributif,-ive adj
convener président[‡] m
conventional conventionnel,-elle adj
conversion into an immovable (property)
immobilisation f
convert fraudently (to) carambouiller v
convert into immovables (to) (property)
immobiliser v
convey (to) transporter[‡] v
conveyance transport[‡] m
convict détenu m, détenue f; réclusionnaire m,f
convict (to) condamner[‡] v; reconnaître v
coupable

conviction condamnation[‡] f
convocation convocation f
coparcener (to be) copartager v (une
succession)
copartner coparticipant,-e adj & m,f
copartnership coparticipation f
copartnership (in); partner in joint account;
coparticipant,-e adj & m,f
copy copie f; exemplaire m
copy or certified copy (of deed, contract
etc) expédition[‡] f
copy (to) copier v
corpse cadavre m
corrupt (to) corrompre[‡] v
corrupt practice abus m
corruption corruption f; vice m
costs dépens[‡] mpl; frais[‡] m,mpl
council conseil[‡] m
council offices; office of mayor mairie f
counsel; lawyer avocat m; avocate f
counsel for the defence défenseur m
counsel formally representing parties before
a commercial court agréé m
counsel representing parties before a Court
of Appeal only avoué m
counseller; counsel conseil[‡] m
count; counting compte m
counter-deed contre-lettre f
counterbalance (to) compenser v
counterfeit (to) contrefaire v
counterfeiting contrefaçon f
counterpart; duplicate double m;
contrepartie f
countersign (to) contresigner v; viser v
countersignature contreseing m
court cour[‡] f; tribunal[‡] m; chambre[‡] f;
conseil[‡] m
court (floor of) prétoire m
court hearing audience[‡] f
Court of Appeal Cour f d'Appel; Cour f de
Cassation
court of summary jurisdiction
correctionnelle f
court sitting or session audience[‡] f
court usher; court porter huissier[‡] m
courts juridiction[‡] f
creditor créancier m, créancière f
crime; (criminal) offence délit[‡] m; crime[‡]
m; criminalité f
criminal criminel,-elle adj; délictuel,-elle adj;

delegate

délictueux,-euse ‡ *adj*
criminal criminel *m*, criminelle *f*;
malfaiteur ‡ *m*
criminal negligence négligence *f* coupable;
négligence *f* criminelle
criminality criminalité *f*
criminalize (to) criminaliser *v*
criminally criminellement *adv*
crippling; damning (eg fault)
rédhibitoire *adj*
cross-examination interrogatoire *m*
culprit coupable ‡ *m,f*
cumulate (to) cumuler *v*
cumulatively cumulativement *adv*
custodial sentence peine *f* privative de
liberté
custody (eg of children after divorce)
garde ‡ *f*
custody; detention détention *f*;
prévention ‡ *f*
custom; usual practice ordinaire ‡ *m*
customs mœurs ‡ *fpl*

D

daily based fine jour-amende *m*
**daily fine for delay in completing contract,
or repaying debt** astreinte *f*
damage dommage ‡ *m*; dégât ‡ *m*;
déprédation; détérioration *f*; les
dégradations *fpl*
damage (to) endommager *v*; léser ‡ *v*
damning (eg fault) rédhibitoire *adj*
date date ‡ *f*
date of payment; date of maturity
échéance ‡ *f*
dation dation ‡ *f*
day jour ‡ *m*
deadline délai ‡ *m*
deal; bargain; contract marché ‡ *m*
death (natural) décès ‡ *m*
debar (to) forclore ‡ *v*
debarment forclusion *f*
debate débat ‡ *m*
debit débit *m*
debt créance ‡ *f*

debtor débiteur ‡ *m*, débitrice ‡ *f*
decease décès ‡ *m*
decease (to) décéder *v*
deceased défunt *m*; de cujus *m*
deception fraude ‡ *f*; tromperie ‡ *f*
decision décision ‡ *f*; jugement ‡ *m*; arrêt *m*
declaration; statement déclaration *f*
declarative déclaratif,-ive *adj*
declaratory déclaratoire *adj*;
déclaratif,-ive *adj*
declare (to) déclarer ‡ *v*; protester *v*
decline (to) décliner *v*
decontrol (to) (eg prices) libérer *v*
decree arrêté *m*; décret *m*
decree (to); order (to) décerner ‡ *v*;
décréter *v*; ordonner *v*
deed acte ‡ *m*
defamation diffamation ‡ *f*
defamatory diffamatoire *adj*;
infamant,-e ‡ *adj*
defame (to) diffamer *v*
default; flaw; fault défaut ‡ *m*
default (in) contumace *f*
default of heirs déshérence ‡ *f*
default(ing); non-appearance défaillance *f*
defaulter; absconder contumace *m,f*
defaulting défaillant,-e *adj*; contumace *adj*
defeasance contre-lettre *f*
defect vice ‡ *m*
defect (due to poor workmanship)
malfaçon *f*
defence défense ‡ *f*
defend (to) défendre ‡ *v*
defendant défendeur *m*, défenderesse *f*;
prévenu *m*, prévenue *f*
defendant (before Appeal Court) intimé *m*,
intimée *f*
defendant (in assize court) accusé *m*,
accusée *f*
defender défenseur *m*
defer (to) reporter ‡ *v*; surseoir ‡ *v*
deferred sursitaire *adj*
deficiency carence *f*; défaut *m*
defraud (to) escroquer *v*; frustrer ‡ *v*
defunct défunt *m*
degradation; debasement dégradation *f*
degree (eg of a university) licence ‡ *f*;
diplôme *m*
delay demeure ‡ *f*; délai ‡ *m*
delegate (to) déléguer *v*

delegation délégation‡ *f*
delegation (of powers, rights)
  subrogation‡ *f*
deliberate déliberé,-e‡ *adj*
delinquency délinquance *f*; criminalité *f*
delinquent coupable *adj*; délictuel,-elle *adj*;
  délinquant,-e‡ *adj*
delinquent délinquant‡ *m*, délinquante‡ *f*;
  coupable *m,f*
deliver a verdict (to) prononcer‡ *v*
deliverance délivrance‡ *f*
delivery envoi *m*; remise‡ *f*
delivery; handing over (of property)
  cession‡ *f*; tradition *f*
demand sommation‡ *f*
demand (to) (eg a penalty) requérir‡ *v*
demand note *(admin)* avertissement *m*
dementia *(med)* démence‡ *f*
demonstration manifestation *f*
demurrage surestarie‡ *f*
denial déni‡ *m*; dénégation‡ *f*
denominate (to) dénommer‡ *v*
deny (to) nier‡ *v*
depart from (to) déroger‡ *v*
dependents charges *fpl* de famille;
  personnes *fpl* à charge
deponent; witness déposant *m*, déposante *f*
deportation order arrêté *m* d'expulsion
deposit arrhes *fpl*; consignation *f*; dépôt‡
  m; versement *m*
deposit (to) déposer‡ *v*
depositary consignataire *m*
depositing; lodgement dépôt *m*
deposition déposition‡ *f*
depositor (of money) déposant *m*,
  déposante *f*
depository dépositaire *m,f*
depot; warehouse dépôt *m*
depredation déprédation *f*
deprivation; deprival privation‡ *f*
derelict (lost object); unclaimed object
  épave *f*
descendant descendant,-e‡ *adj*;
  descendant‡ *m*, descendante‡ *f*
descendants filiation‡ *f*
desecration violation‡ *f*
desert (to) abandonner *v*
desertion (of home, wife, husband)
  abandon‡ *m*
designate (to) dénommer‡ *v*; désigner *v*

designation appellation *f*; dénomination *f*;
  désignation *f*
desire; willingness volonté‡ *f*
despite; in spite of nonobstant *prep & adv*
destination destination‡ *f*
destruction anéantissement *m*
details renseignement‡ *m*
detention détention‡ *f*
deterioration détérioration *f*
detrimental; injurious dommageable *adj*
development (of events) déroulement *m*
devise (to) léguer *v*; inventer *v*
devisee légataire *m,f*
devolution dévolution *f*
die (to) mourir *v*; décéder *v*
difference of opinion différend‡ *m*
diffuse (to) diffuser *v*
diminished atténué,-e *adj*
din tapage‡ *m*
diploma; certificate brevet *m*; diplôme *m*
directive; instruction instruction‡ *f*
disability inhabilité‡ *f*; invalidité‡ *f*;
  incapacité‡ *f*
disabled invalide *adj*
disabled person handicapé *m*, handicapée *f*
disagreement différend‡ *m*
disappearance disparition *f*
disaster sinistre‡ *m*
disbanding dissolution *f*
discharge (to) décharger‡ *v*; renvoyer‡ *v*
discharge; discharging décharge‡ *f*
disciplinary disciplinaire‡ *adj*
disclosure divulgation *f*
discrimination discrimination‡ *f*
discussion débat‡ *m*
disease maladie‡ *f*
disencumbrance (of a mortgage)
  dégrèvement *m*
dismiss (to) absoudre *v*; congédier *v*;
  démettre *v*
dismiss (to) (eg employee) renvoyer‡ *v*;
  licencier *v*
dismiss / reject a suit (to) débouter *v*
dismissal (of case, when defendant is
considered to have no case to answer)
  absolution *f*
dismissal (of employee) licenciement‡ *m*
dispensary officine *f*
dispenser of justice justicier *m*, justicière *f*
displacement; transfer déplacement *m*

disposal (of a business, etc) expédition[‡] *f*
disposal disposition[‡] *f*
dispose (to) disposer de[‡] *v*
disposition disposition[‡] *f*
dispossession éviction *f*
dispute conflit[‡] *m*; contestation[‡] *f*;
  différend[‡] *m*; litige[‡] *m*
disqualified (from inheriting) indigne[‡] *adj*
disqualify (to) inhabiliter[‡] *v*; rendre *v*
  inhabile
disseisin; dispossession dessaisissement *m*
dissimulation; dissembling dissimulation *f*
dissolution (marriage, partnership, etc)
  dissolution *f*
dissolve (to) (marriage, partnership, etc)
  dissoudre *v*
distortion distorsion *f*
distrain (to) saisir[‡] *v*
distrainee; person distrained saisi *m*
distrainer saisissant,-e *adj*; saisissant *m*
distraining saisissant,-e *adj*
distraint saisie-arrêt[‡] *f*; mainmise *f*;
  exécution[‡] *f*; saisie[‡] *f*
distribution répartition[‡] *f*
disturbance émeute *f*; trouble[‡] *m*
diversion divertissement *m*
divide (to) partager *v*; séparer *v*
divide into lots (to); share out (to) (eg
estate) lotir *v*
dividing into lots; parcelling out
  lotissement *m*
division; sharing; partition (of real property)
  partage[‡] *m*
divorce divorce[‡] *m*
divorce (to) divorcer[‡] *v*
divulgence divulgation *f*
dock banc *m* des accusés; box *m* des
  accusés
document; written document écrit *m*;
  pièce *f*
documentation dossier[‡] *m*
dolus malus dol *m*
domain domaine[‡] *m*
domicile domicile[‡] *m*; demeure[‡] *f*
donation don[‡] *m*; donation[‡] *f*
donee donataire *m,f*
donor donateur *m*, donatrice *f*
dormant dormant,-e[‡] *adj*
dossier dossier[‡] *m*
double double *m*

down payment (of annuity on a property)
  bouquet *m*
dowry dot *f*
draft (to) minuter[‡] *v*; rédiger *v*
draft of a contract minute[‡] *f*; projet[‡] *m*
drafting rédaction[‡] *f*
draw up (to) dresser[‡] *v*; établir[‡] *v*;
  minuter[‡] *v*; rédiger[‡] *v*; instrumenter *v*
drawing up confection[‡] *f*; rédaction[‡] *f*;
  passation[‡] *f*
driving conduite[‡] *f*
drug drogue[‡] *f*; stupéfiant *m*
due date; expiry; settlement date
  échéance[‡] *f*
due dû, due[‡] *adj*
duplicate duplicata *m,inv*; double *m*
duration durée *f*
duress contrainte[‡] *f*
duty devoir[‡] *m*; obligation[‡] *f*
duty droit[‡] *m*; taxe *f*
duty; duties; due, dues droit *m*
dwelling house; accommodation logement[‡]
  m; habitation[‡] *f*

E

earnings gains[‡] *mpl*; revenu *m*; salaire *m*
easement servitude[‡] *f*
education enseignment *m*; instruction *f*
effect fictitiously (to) (eg sale, contract)
  simuler[‡] *v*
effect effet[‡] *m*
either... or... soit... soit... *conj*
emancipate (to) émanciper *v*
emancipation émancipation *f*
embezzlement détournement[‡] *m*; déprédation *f*; malversation *f*
emolument dotation *f*
emoluments émoluments *mpl*
employee employé *m*, employée *f*
employer employeur *m*; mandant *m*,
  mandante *f*
employment emploi[‡] *m*
employment usage *m*
enable (to); empower (to) habiliter[‡] *v*
enacting terms (of a statute, etc)
  dispositif *m*

enclosed ci-inclus *adj*
encumber (to) (building) grever *v*
encumbrance servitude‡ *f*
end fin‡ *f*
endeavour tentative‡ *f*
endorse (to); guarantee (to) avaliser *v*
endorse (to); sanction (to) homologuer *v*
endorsement avenant *m*
endow (to) (eg institution) doter *v*
endowment dotation *f*
enforce (to) (eg law, writ, etc) exécuter‡ *v*
enforceable *adj* **(of decree, contract, etc)** exécutoire‡ *adj*
enforcement (eg of law) exécution‡ *f*
enforcer exécuteur *m*, exécutrice *f*
engage (to) (staff etc) embaucher *v*; engager *v*
engagement engagement *m*
enjoyment jouissance‡ *f*
enrol inscrire‡ *v*
enrolment inscription‡ *f*
ensure (to) assurer *v*
entail (to) (an estate) grever‡ *v*; substituer *v*
entailed (estate) inaliénable *adj*; indisponible *adj*
enter (to); note (to) enregistrer‡ *v*
entering into (contract, lease) passation‡ *f*
entirely; fairly bel et bien *adv*
entitled; qualified; competent capable *adj*
entrust (to) charger‡ *v*
entry (into accounts ledger) passation‡ *f*
enumerate (to) articuler *v*
enumeration articulation *f*
equal representation on both sides (with) paritaire *adj*
equality égalité‡ *f*
erasure rature‡ *f*
error erreur‡ *f*; faute‡ *f*
escape évasion *f*
escape (to) échapper‡ *v*
escheat déshérence‡ *f*
espionage espionnage‡ *m*
establish (to) constater *v*; établir‡ *v*; instituer‡ *v*
establishing établissement‡ *m*
establishment (eg of fact) constatation‡ *f*
establishment établissement‡ *m*
estate biens *mpl*; domaine‡ *m*; fonds‡ *m*; propriété *f*; succession‡ *f*

estate agency Immobilière *f*
estimate devis‡ *m*
estimated; supposed supposé,-e *adj*
estop (to) forclore‡ *v*
European Court of Justice Cour *f* Européenne de Justice
event circonstance *f*; événement *m*; fait‡ *m*
evict (to) évincer *v*
eviction éviction *f*
evidence preuve‡ *f*; déposition‡ *f*; témoignage‡ *m*
examination (eg of witness) audition *f*; interrogatoire‡ *m*
examine (to); investigate (to) (a case) enquêter *v*; informer *v*; instruire‡ *v*
examining magistrate juge *m* d'instruction; magistrat *m* instructeur
except; but; save sauf‡ *prep*
exception exception‡ *f*
excess excès‡ *m*
excitation excitation *f*
exclusion exclusion‡ *f*
exclusive exclusif,-ive‡ *adj*; privatif,-ive‡ *adj*
execute (to) exécuter‡ *v*
execution exécution‡ *f*; saisie‡ *f*
executor, executrix exécuteur‡ *m*, exécutrice‡ *f*
executory exécutoire‡ *adj*
exemplar exemplaire *m*
exemption exemption *f*; dégrèvement‡ *m*
exercise (to) exercer‡ *v*; lever *v*
exert (to) exercer‡ *v*
exhaustion anéantissement *m*
exhumation exhumation‡ *f*
expect (to) prévoir‡ *v*
expenses; expenditure charges *fpl*; frais‡ *m,mpl*
expert expert‡ *m*
expert valuation / appraisal expertise‡ *f*
expiration expiration‡ *f*; échéance *f*
expiration of tenancy échéance‡ *f*
explanation éclaircissement‡ *m*; explication *f*
explicit explicite *adj*; exprès,-esse *adj*
explicitly explicitement *adv*; expressément *adv*
exploit exploit‡ *m*
explosive explosif *m*

express (to) exprimer *v*; énoncer *v*; traduire *v*
express exprès,-esse *adj*
expressly expressément *adv*
expropriation expropriation *f*
expulsion exclusion *f*
extension of payment period prorogation[‡] *f*
extension of time prorogation[‡] *f*
extinction extinction[‡] *f*; défaillance *f*
extinguish (to) éteindre[‡] *v*
extortion extorsion *f*

F

fact fait[‡] *m*
factor affactureur *m*
factoring affacturage *m*
faculty faculté[‡] *f*
failing; faltering défaillant,-e *adj*
failure faillite[‡] *f*; manquement[‡] *m*; déconfiture *f*
failure to appear in court non-comparution *f*
failure to observe (orders, etc) inobservation *f*
faith foi[‡] *f*
fake; forged faux[‡], fausse[‡] *adj*
fake; forgery faux[‡] *m*
fall due (to) (eg rent) échoir[‡] *v*
fall; decline déchéance[‡] *f*
fallen déchu,-e[‡] *adj* [p.p of déchoir]
falling due; payable échéant *adj*
false imprisonment séquestration *f*
false faux[‡], fausse[‡] *adj*
falsehood faux[‡] *m*
farm lease ferme[‡] *f*
farm rent; rent paid for use of arable land fermage *m*
farm, farmhouse ferme[‡] *f*
father père[‡] *m*
fault défaut[‡] *m*; faute[‡] *f*; tort[‡] *m*; vice[‡] *m*
fault; defect (due to poor workmanship) malfaçon *f*
fee(s); honorarium honoraires[‡] *mpl*; frais[‡] *m,mpl*; redevance[‡] *f*
feign (to) affecter *v*; simuler[‡] *v*
felony crime *m*
fence receleur *m*, receleuse *f*

fiduciarily fiduciairement *adv*
fiduciary fiduciaire[‡] *adj*
fief fief *m*
file dossier[‡] *m*
file (to); lodge (to); register (to) déposer[‡] *v*
filiation filiation[‡] *f*
filing (of return at registration office) passation[‡] *f*
final conveyance document acte *m* authentique; acte *m* définitive; acte *m* de vente
find (to) (lost object, treasure etc) inventer *v*
finder (of lost object, treasure, etc) inventeur *m*, inventrice *f*
finding (of lost object, treasure, etc) invention[‡] *f*
findings conclusion[‡] *f*
fine amende[‡] *f*
fine; parking fine; parking ticket contravention[‡] *f*
fingerprint empreinte[‡] *f* digitale
fire outbreak incendie *m*
firearm arme *f*
firm entreprise[‡] *f*; société[‡] *f*
fiscality fiscalité[‡] *f*
fit to; fit for; apte *adj*
fit capable *adj*; habile[‡] *adj*
fitness; capacity aptitude *f*
fitting; fit idoine[‡] *adj*
fix (to) arrêter *v*
fix (to) (eg price) établir[‡] *v*
fixed inamovible[‡] *adj*
fixed rate; fixed price; forfait[‡] *m*
fixity of tenure inamovibilité *f*
fixtures and fittings équipments *mpl*
flaw; fault; defect défaut[‡] *m*; vice[‡] *m*
folded cover pli[‡] *m*
folly folie *f*
footprint empreinte[‡] *f* (de pied)
forbid (to); prohibit (to) défendre *v*
force; strength force *f*
fore-mentioned prénommé *m*, prénommée *f*
foreclose (to) (a mortgage) forclore[‡] *v*
foreclosure saisie[‡] *f*; forclusion *f*
foreign; strange étranger,-ère *adj*
foreigner; stranger étranger *m*, étrangère *f*
foresee (to) prévoir[‡] *v*
forfeit; penalty (for breaking a contract, etc) dédit[‡] *m*

forfeiture confiscation *f*
forfeiture (of rights, etc) déchéance[‡] *f*
forge (to) contrefaire *v*; falsifier *v*
forger; counterfeiter contrefacteur *m*
forgery contrefaçon *f*; faux[‡] *m*
forgiveness pardon[‡] *m*
form forme[‡] *f*; mode *m*
formal deed (of sale) acte *m* de vente
formal demand mise *f* en demeure
formality; formal procedure formalité *f*
formation formation[‡] *f*
forwarding agent transporteur[‡] *m*
foul play malveillance[‡] *f*
foundation fondement[‡] *m*
founder fondateur[‡] *m*, fondatrice[‡] *f*
framework cadre *m*
frank; straightforward franc[‡], franche[‡] *adj*
fraud escroquerie[‡] *f*; dol[‡] *m*; fraude[‡] *f*; tromperie[‡] *f*
fraudulent dolosif,-ive *adj*
fraudulent misrepresentation dol[‡] *m*
fraudulent conversion carambouillage *m*; carambouille *f*
fraudulent use of a third party's identity as one's own interposition *f*
free (to) libérer *v*
free pardon grâce[‡] *f*
free franc[‡], franche[‡] *adj*; libre[‡] *adj*
freedom liberté[‡] *f*
frustrate (to) frustrer[‡] *v*
fund masse[‡] *f*
funds fonds[‡] *m*
furniture mobilier[‡] *m*; meuble[‡] *m*

giving up dessaisissement *m*
go to court (to) plaider[‡] *v*; ester *v* en justice
golden handshake dessous-de-table *m*
good(s) bien *m*, biens *mpl*
goodwill (of business) pas *m* de porte
grace grâce[‡] *f*
graduate (of a university) diplomé *m*, diplomée *f*; licencié *m*, licenciée *f*
graffiti graffiti *mpl*
grant aide *f*; dotation *f*; subvention[‡] *f*
grant (to) (eg right) impartir[‡] *v*
grantee (eg of diploma) impétrant *m*, impétrante *f*
granting octroi[‡] *m*
grantor cédant *m*, cédante *f*
grantor (of annuity or dowry) constituant *m*
gratitude reconnaissance[‡] *f*
gratuity gratification *f*
ground motif[‡] *m*; cause *f*; moyen *m*
guarantee caution[‡] *f*; garantie[‡] *f*; sûreté *f*; garant *m*
guarantee (to) garantir[‡] *v*
guarantor; surety garant[‡] *m*, garante [‡]*f*
guard (to) garder[‡] *v*
guardian tuteur[‡] *m*, tutrice[‡] *f*
guardian tutélaire[‡] *adj*
guardianship tutelle[‡] *f*; garde[‡] *f*; curatelle *f*
guilty coupable[‡] *adj*

H

G

gain; winning gain[‡] *m*
get a divorce (to) divorcer *v*
gift don[‡] *m*; donation[‡] *f*; liberalité *f*
give a grant to (to) (eg university) doter *v*
give evidence (to) témoigner[‡] (de) *v*; déposer[‡] *v*
give up (to) renoncer[‡] *v*; céder[‡] *v*; se dessaisir *v*
given or considering (the circumstances) attendu[‡] *prep*

habitual offender récidiviste *m,f*
haggle over (to); bargain over (to) marchander *v*
haggler marchandeur *m*, marchandeuse *f*
handing over remise *f*
handling gestion[‡] *f*
hanging; pending pendant,-e[‡] *adj*
harassment harcèlement[‡] *m*
harbour (to) (criminal) receler *v*
harbouring (of criminal) recel *m*; recelé *m*; recèlement *m*
harm dommage *m*; tort *m*
harm (to); prejudice (to) nuire[‡] *v*
haulage contractor transporteur[‡] *m*

have (at one's disposal) (to) disposer de‡ v
head office siege m
head chef m
hear (to) (eg witness) ouïr v
hear (to) entendre‡ v; écouter v
hearing débats‡ mpl
hearing (of witnesses) audition f;
   témoignage‡ m
hearing in camera à huis m clos
heart fond‡ m
heavy; substantial (eg damages)
   élevé,-e‡ adj
heir, heiress héritier‡ m, héritière‡ f;
   légataire m,f
henceforth; hereafter dorénavant adv
heredity hérédité‡ f
hereinafter ci-après adv
herewith ci-inclus adj; ci-joint adj
heritage patrimoine m
high (eg damages) élevé,-e‡ adj
higher bid; higher offer suroffre f
hindrance entrave‡ f
hiring louage‡ m; location‡ f
hold an inquiry (to) enquêter‡ v
hold back (to) retenir‡ v
holder (of right, title, certificate etc)
   titulaire‡ m,f
holding (of securities, etc) détention‡ f
home maison‡ f
homicidal homicide‡ adj
homicide homicide‡ m
homologation homologation f
honest propre adj
hostage otage‡ m
hour heure‡ f
house habitation‡ f; maison‡ f
house search perquisition f
housebreaking cambriolage m par
   effraction
housing estate or site; housing
   development lotissement m
husband mari m; époux m
hypothecation nantissement‡ m
hypothetical hypothétique adj

I

ignominious; dishonourable
   infamant,-e‡ adj
illegal illégal adj; illicite‡ adj
illegal restraint séquestration f
illegal subcontracting of labour
   marchandage m
illicit illicite‡ adj
illness maladie‡ f
imbalance distorsion f
immobilization immobilisation f
immobilize (to) immobiliser v
immovable immeuble adj
immunity immunité‡ f
immunity from seizure or distraint
   insaisissabilité f
impediment empêchement‡ m
implementation; implementing (regulation)
   mise f en œuvre
implication sous-entendu m
implied tacite‡ adj
imprescriptibility imprescriptibilité f
imprescriptible imprescriptible adj
impression; imprint empreinte‡ f
imprisonment emprisonnement‡ m;
   incarcération f; réclusion‡ f
improper solicitation of a legacy captation f
improvidence imprévision f
imprudence imprudence‡ f
impugn (to) (eg evidence) récuser‡ v
imputability imputabilité f
in abeyance (eg inheritance) vacant,-e‡ adj
in accordance with selon prep
in force en vigueur‡ f
in front of; round the front
   par-devant‡ adv
in receipt of (state) assistance (person)
   assisté m, assistée f
in the hands of par-devers‡ prep
in trust fiduciairement adv
inadmissibility inadmissibilité f
inadmissible inadmissible adj;
   irrecevable‡ adj
inalienability inaliénabilité f
inalienable (property) inaliénable adj;
   indisponible adj
inaptitude inaptitude f

incapability incapacité[‡] *f*
incapable *adj* incapable[‡] *adj*; inhabile[‡] *adj*
incapable person incapable[‡] *m,f*
incapacity incapacité[‡] *f*; inhabilité[‡] *f*
incarceration incarcération *f*
incest inceste *m*
incestuous incestueux,-euse[‡] *adj*
incident incident[‡] *m*; circonstance *f*
incidental incident,-e *adj*
incidental plea (of defence) exception[‡] *f*
incitement; inciting incitation[‡] *f*; excitation[‡] *f*
income revenu[‡] *m*; rente[‡] *f*
incompatibility incompatibilité *f*
incompetence nullité[‡] *f*; incapacité[‡] *f*; incompétence[‡] *f*
incompetent incapable[‡] *adj*; incompétent,-e *adj*
incontestable inopposable *adj*
increase in value; increment value; appreciation plus-value[‡] *f*
increase; growth accroissement *m*
indefeasibility inaliénabilité *f*; imprescriptibilité *f*
indefeasible imprescriptible *adj*
indemnify (to) indemniser[‡] *v*
indemnity indemnité[‡] *f*
index; rating indice *m*
indication; sign indice *m*
indict (to) mettre en accusation[‡] *f*
indictable offence crime[‡] *m*
indictment accusation[‡] *f*; inculpation *f*
indirect (eg tax, line of descent) indirect,-e *adj*
indisputable irréfutable *adj*
individual personne[‡] *f*
individualization individualisation[‡] *f*
individualize (to) individualiser *v*
indivisibility indivisibilité *f*
industrial disease maladie *f* professionnelle
ineffectiveness; inefficacy inefficacité[‡] *f*
inept; clumsy inhabile *adj*
infancy (legal) minorité[‡] *f*
infant enfant[‡] *m*
inform (to) instruire[‡] *v*; informer[‡] *v*
informant déclarant *m*, déclarante *f*
information technology informatique[‡] *f*
information renseignement[‡] *m*; information[‡] *f*
infraction infraction[‡] *f*

infringement contravention *f*; contrefaçon *f*; atteinte[‡] *f*; infraction[‡] *f*
inherit (to); succeed to (to) hériter[‡] *v*; succéder à *v*
inheritance héritage[‡] *m*; succession[‡] *f*; hoirie *f*; patrimoine[‡] *m*
initial (to) (document) parapher *v*; viser *v*
initials (of one's name) paraphe *m*
injunction injonction[‡] *f*; avant faire droit *m,inv*; avant dire droit *m,inv*; arrêt de suspension[‡] *f*
injure (to) léser[‡] *v*
injurious dommageable *adj*
injury lésion[‡] *f*; injure[‡] *f*; dommage[‡] *m*; préjudice *m*; tort *m*
innocent innocent,-e *adj*
innocent person innocent *m*, innocente *f*
inobservance inobservation *f*
inquest (on a dead person) enquête[‡] *f*
inquire into (to) (eg crime) informer[‡] *v*
inquiry enquête[‡] *f*; information[‡] *f*
inquisitorial inquisitoire[‡] *adj*
insanity; madness démence[‡] *f*; aliénation *f* mentale
inscription inscription[‡] *f*
insecure précaire[‡] *adj*
insert (to) introduire[‡] *v*
insolvency déconfiture *f*; faillite[‡] *f*; carence *f*
inspection vu[‡] *m*
instance; circumstance cas *m*
institute (to) introduire[‡] *v*; instituer[‡] *v*
institute proceedings (to) (against someone) intenter *v* (une action, un procès à, contre quelqu'un); engager[‡] *v*
institution institution *f*
instruction or brief (to examining magistrate) réquisitoire *m*
instructor instructeur[‡] *m*
instrument; title acte[‡] *m*
draw up a formal document (to) (eg deed, contract) instrumenter *v*
insult outrage[‡] *m*; injure[‡] *f*
insurance assurance[‡] *f*
insurance agent; insurance company assureur *m*
intended purpose (of building, sum of money etc) destination[‡] *f*
intention intention[‡] *f*; propos[‡] *m*
interdependence solidarité *f*

interdependent solidaire‡ adj
interdiction interdiction‡ f
interfering (sexual); molesting
   attouchement m
interim order avant faire droit m,inv; avant
   dire droit m,inv
interjection interjection‡ f
interposition interposition f
interrogate (to) interroger v
interrogation interrogation f; interro-
   gatoire‡ m
interruption interruption‡ f
intervene (to) intervenir‡ v
intervener; intermediate intervenant m,
   intervenante f
intervention intervention‡ f; interposition f
intestate intestat‡ adj
intimidation intimidation f; menace‡ f
intimidation (of a witness) subornation‡ f
intoxication ivresse‡ f
intransmissibility intransmissibilité f
intransmissible intransmissible adj
introduce (to) (eg tax) instituer‡ v;
   introduire‡ v
invalid (eg will); null and void invalide adj
invalidate (to) invalider v; vicier v; infirmer v
invalidating infirmatif,-ive adj
invalidation infirmation f
invalidity (eg of marriage, deed) nullité‡ f
inveigler captateur m, captatrice f
inveigling captation f
invent (to) inventer v
invention invention‡ f
inventiveness invention‡ f
inventor inventeur m, inventrice f
inventory inventaire‡ m
inventory (to) inventorier v
invest (to) investir‡ v
investigate (to) (eg crime) informer‡ v;
   enquêter‡ v; instruire‡ v
investigation enquête‡ f; instruction‡ f
investment; supply apport m
invoke (to) invoquer‡ v
irrebuttable irréfragable adj
irrefutable irréfutable adj
irregular irrégulier,-ière‡ adj
irremovability inamovibilité f
irremovable inamovible adj
irresponsability irresponsabilité f
irrevocability irrévocabilité f

isolation of infected animals séquestration f
issue a writ (to) (against someone); serve a
   writ (to) (on someone) assigner v
issue; delivery délivrance‡ f
issue (to) délivrer v
item in contract stipulation‡ f;
   prescription‡ f
iterative itératif,-ive adj

J

jargon jargon‡ m
job; employment occupation‡ f; emploi‡ m
joining; joinder jonction‡ f
joint (eg owner, estate) indivis,-e‡ adj
joint; conjoined conjoint,-e‡ adj
joint and several solidaire‡ adj
joint and several liability solidarité f
joint holder codétenteur m, codétentrice f
joint obligor cooblige m; coobligée f
joint owner indivisaire m,f
joint ownership; joint possession
   indivision‡ f; en communauté‡ f
jointly conjointement‡ adv; indivisément‡
   adv; solidairement adv
jointly liable; binding on all parties
   solidaire‡ adj
judge juge‡ m
judge (to) juger‡ v
judge of appeal conseiller m à la cour
   d'appel (ou Cour de Cassation)
judge's order; judgment; ruling
   ordonnance‡ f
judgement arrêt‡ m; condamnation‡ f;
   jugement‡ m
judicial judiciaire‡ adj; juridique‡ adj
junction jonction‡ f
juridicial juridique‡ adj
jurisdiction compétence‡ f; juridiction‡ f;
   ressort‡ m
jurisprudence juridisprudence f
juror juré m
jury jury‡ m
jury box banc m du jury; banc m des jurés
justice justice‡ f
justiciable justiciable‡ adj; légitime adj

justifiable légitime *adj*
justified fondé,-e[‡] *adj*
juvenile delinquency criminalité *f* juvénile

K

keep (to) garder[‡] *v*
keeping maintien *m*
key money (flat) pas *m* de porte
kidnapping rapt[‡] *m*; enlèvement *m*
knock coup *m*

L

lack of authority; lack of jurisdiction
  incompétence *f*
lack of foresight imprévision *f*
lack of funds; insolvency carence *f*
lack manquement[‡] *m*
lady dame *f*
land registry cadastre *m*; bureau *m* du
  cadastre; conservation *f* des hypothèques
land; estate propriété[‡] *f*; fonds[‡] *m*
landlord; landlady propriétaire[‡] *m,f*
lapse défaillance *f*
lapse (to) périmer[‡] *v*; devenir *v* caduc
lapse of offer caducité *f*
lapsing caducité *f*
larceny by a baillee carambouillage *m*;
  carambouille *f*
later postérieur *adj*
laundering (eg of money) blanchiment *m*
law droit[‡] *m*; loi[‡] *f*
law courts palais[‡] *m*
law degree (equivalent to LL.B) maîtrise *f*
  en droit
lawful legal,-e[‡] *adj*; légitime[‡] *adj*
lawfully légitimement *adv*
lawsuit affaire *f*; action[‡] *f*; litige[‡] *m*;
  poursuite[‡] *f*; procès *m*
lawyer avocat[‡] *m*; avocate *f*; conseiller *m*
  juridique; conseillère *f* juridique
lay out (to) (eg conditions) établir *v*
lease bail[‡] *m*; baux *mpl*

leaseback cession-bail *f*
leaseholder locataire[‡] *m,f* à bail; preneur
  m, preneuse *f*
leave congé[‡] *m*
leave (to) laisser[‡] *v*
leave a trust (to) fidéicommisser *v*
legacy legs[‡] *m*
legal judiciaire[‡] *adj*; légal,-e *adj*;
  juridique[‡] *adj*
legal act of giving or conferring (eg
  guardianship) dation *f*
legal adviser conseiller *m* juridique[‡];
  conseillère *f* juridique
legal competency capacité[‡] *f*
legal department contentieux[‡] *m*
legal document acte[‡] *m*
legal guardianship curatelle *f*
legal incapacity inhabilité[‡] *f*
legal norm norme *f*
legal notice (of steps about to be taken);
  denunciation dénonciation *f*
legal proceedings instance[‡] *f*
legal successor; assign; assignee
  ayant-droit *m*; ayant-cause *m*
legatee héritier[‡] *m*, héritière[‡] *f*;
  légataire[‡] *m,f*
legitimacy légitimité *f*
legitimate légitime[‡] *adj*; valable[‡] *adj*
legitimately légitimement *adv*
legitimation (eg of child) légitimation *f*
legitimate (to) légaliser *v*; reconnaître *v*
lending; loaning (of money) prestation[‡] *f*
length durée *f*
leniency indulgence *f*
lenient indulgent *adj*
lesion lésion *f*
lessee locataire[‡] *m,f*; locataire[‡] *m,f* à bail;
  preneur *m*, preneuse *f*
lessor bailleur *m*, bailleresse *f*; locateur *m*;
  locatrice *f*
let (to); allow (to) laisser[‡] *v*
let go (to) dessaisir[‡] *v*
letter lettre *f*; pli[‡] *m*
letter of credit lettre *f* de crédit; créance *f*
letters patent; patent brevet *m*
letting (eg house) location[‡] *f*; louage[‡] *m*
levy impôt *m*
levying (eg tax) levée[‡] *f*
liability responsabilité *f*; engagement[‡] *m*
liable responsable[‡] *adj*; assujetti[‡] *adj*

libel diffamation *f*; calomnie *f*
libel (to) diffamer‡ *v*
libellous diffamatoire *adj*
liberality liberalité *f*
liberate (to) émanciper *v*
liberation émancipation *f*; libération‡ *f*
liberty liberté‡ *f*
licence permis‡ *m*; licence‡ *f*
licensee licencié *m*, licenciée *f*
life vie‡ *f*
life annuity viager‡ *m*; rente *f* viagère
life interest ‡usufruit *m*
life interest; for life viager,-ère *adj*
lift (to) lever‡ *v*
lift up again (to) relever‡ *v*
lifting levée‡ *f*
limited to (to be) se borner *v* à
liquidate (to); wind up (to) (eg business, company) liquider‡ *v*
liquidator liquidateur‡ *m*, liquidatrice‡ *f*
liquidity liquidité‡ *f*
listen to (to) entendre‡ *v*
litigant plaideur *m*, plaideuse *f*; partie‡ *f*; justiciable *m,f*
litigate (to) plaider‡ *v*
litigation litige‡ *m*; contentieux‡ *m*
litigious person plaideur *m*, plaideuse *f*
live together (to) cohabiter *v*
livestock cheptel‡ *m*
living person vif‡ *m*
living with somebody cohabitation *f*
load charge *f*
loan emprunt‡ *m*; prêt‡ *m*
local administrative office mairie *f*
located sis, sise *adj*
lodge (to) (eg document) déposer‡ *v*
lodge an appeal (to) interjeter *v* appel
lodgement; filing dépôt *m*
lodger locataire‡ *m,f*
lodging logement‡ *m*
lodging of an appeal interjection‡ *f*
look after (to) garder *v*
look for (to); research (to) rechercher *v*
lose a case (to) succomber *v*
losing party (in a lawsuit) perdant *m*
loss dommage *m*; dechéance‡ *f*

M

madness folie *f*; démence *f*
magistracy magistrature‡ *f*
magistrate magistrat‡ *m*
magistrates court correctionnelle‡ *f*; tribunal *m* correctionel
magistrature magistrature‡ *f*
maintenance entretien *m*; maintien *m*; aliments *mpl*; pension *f* alimentaire
major; of age majeur,-e‡ *adj & m,f*
majority majorité‡ *f*
make a complaint (to) se plaindre‡ *v*
make a copy of (to) copier *v*
make a stocklist of (to) inventorier *v*
make a trust (to) fidéicommisser *v*
make an inventory of (to) inventorier *v*
make one's will (to) tester‡ *v*
make out (to) (eg document, lease, invoice, cheque) rédiger‡ *v*
making of rules; regulating; control réglementation‡ *f*
making; construction; preparation confection *f*
maladministration forfaiture *f*; malversations *fpl*
malevolence; spite malveillance‡ *f*
malice aforethought préméditation *f*
malpractice; cheating malfaçon *f*
management gestion‡ *f*
manager dirigeant *m*
mandate; mandamus order mandement *m*
mandate; warrant mandat‡ *m*
mandator mandant *m*, mandante *f*
mandatory impératif,-ve *adj*; obligatoire‡ *adj*
manner façon‡ *f*
manners mœurs‡ *fpl*
marital marital,-e‡ *adj*
mark marc‡ *m*
marked; pronounced prononcé,-e‡ *adj*
market marché‡ *m*
marriage mariage‡ *m*; (see also lit *m*)
marriage settlement in favour of daughter dot *f*
mass masse‡ *f*
master maître‡ *m* (title of address given to lawyers, notaries, etc)

material matière[‡] *f*
maternity maternité[‡] *f*
matter matière[‡] *f*
matters in dispute; litigation contentieux *m*
maximum maximum *adj & m*
maximum sentence maximum *adj & m*
mean (to) signifier[‡] *v*
means moyen[‡] *m*
meaning signification[‡] *f*
memorandum mémoire[‡] *f*
memory mémoire[‡] *f*
menace menace[‡] *f*
mental disorder démence *f*
message message *m*
method mode *m*; modalité[‡] *f*
minimum *adj* minimum[‡] *adj & m*,
   minimums *pl*, minima *pl*
minimum sentence minimum *adj & m*,
   minimums *pl*, minima *pl*
minor; under age mineur,-e[‡] *adj*;
   impubère *adj*
minor; young person under 18 mineur[‡]
   m,f; impubère *m,f*
minority minorité[‡] *f*
minute (written record) minute[‡] *f*
minute; moment minute[‡] *f*
minutes (of a meeting) procès-verbal[‡] *m*;
   procès-verbaux *mpl*
misappropriation divertissement[‡] *m*;
   détournement[‡] *m*; déprédation *f*;
   distraction[‡] *f*
misdemeanour délit[‡] *m*
missing person absent *m*, absente *f*
   (also *adj*)
mistake erreur[‡] *f*; méprise[‡] *f*; faute[‡] *f*
mitigation atténuation *f*; mitigation *f*;
   réduction *f*
modality; means; way modalité[‡] *f*
mode façon[‡] *f*; mode *m*; modalité[‡] *f*
moderation; restraint modération[‡] *f*
molesting attouchement *m*
money order mandat[‡] *m*
morals mœurs[‡] *fpl*
moratorium moratoire *m*; moratorium *m*
moratory moratoire[‡] *adj*
mortgage hypothèque[‡] *f*
mortgage (to) (property) hypothéquer *v*
mortgage office and land registry bureau *m*
   des hypothèques
mother mère[‡] *f*

motive motif[‡] *m*
movable meuble[‡] *m* (also *adj*)
movable; transferable mobilier,-ière[‡] *adj*
mugging agression *f*
murder meurtre[‡] *m*; crime[‡] *m*; homicide[‡]
   m; assassinat *m*
murder attempt attentat[‡] *m*
murdered homicidé,-e[‡] *adj*
murderer / murderess meurtrier *m*,
   meurtrière *f*; criminel *m*, criminelle *f*
mutability mutabilité *f*
mutation mutation[‡] *f*
mutual aid entraide[‡] *f* (no *pl*)

N

name (to); designate (to) dénommer *v*
narcotic stupéfiant *m*
nationality nationalité[‡] *f*; origine *f*
neglect (to) délaisser[‡] *v*
neglect; state of neglect délaissement[‡] *m*
negligence négligence[‡] *f*; faute[‡] *f*;
   imprudence[‡] *f*
negotiability (eg of pension) cessibilité *f*
negotiable (of pension, etc) cessible *adj*
negotiate (to) négocier *v*
negotiation négociation *f*
negotiator interlocuteur[‡] *m*, interlocu-
   trice[‡] *f*
nevertheless nonobstant[‡] *prep & adv*
news information[‡] *f*
next-of-kin héritier *m*, héritière *f*
nil nul, nulle[‡] *adj*
no ground for prosecution non-lieu[‡] *m*
non-accountability irresponsabilité *f*
non-assistance non-assistance[‡] *f*
non-existant nul, nulle[‡] *adj*
non-invocability inopposabilité *f*
non-invocable inopposable *adj*
non-observance inobservation *f*
non-performance (eg contract) inexécution *f*
non-productive land etc non-valeur *f*
non-seizability insaisissabilité *f*
non-seizable insaisissable *adj*
non-transferability intransmissibilité *f*
non-transferable intransmissible *adj*

nonage minorité[‡] *f*
nonappearance non-comparution *f*;
   défaillance *f*; défaut *m* de comparution
nonenjoyment non-jouissance *f*
nonretroactivity non-rétroactivité *f*
nonsuit; nonsuiting débouté *m*;
   déboutement *m*
nonsuit (to) débouter *v*
not available; unavailable indisponible *adj*
not distrainable insaisissable *adj*
not observed (rules, etc) inobservé,-e *adj*
not owed, not due (money) indu[‡] *adj*
not qualified (to try case) incompétent,-e
   adj
notary; notary public; solicitor
   (conveyancing) notaire *m*
note down (to) inscrire[‡] *v*
notice avertissement *m*; notification[‡] *f*;
   intimation[‡] *f*
notice of dismissal, discharge or
   non-continuance congé[‡] *m*
notice of termination (eg of partnership)
   dénonciation *f*
notification signification[‡] *f*; intimation[‡] *f*;
   notification[‡] *f*
notification to attend (written)
   convocation *f*
notify (to) intimer[‡] *v*; signifier[‡] *v*
notwithstanding nonobstant[‡] *prep & adv*
novation novation *f*
null and void caduc, caduque *adj*; nul,
   nulle[‡] *adj*
nullifying infirmatif,-ive *adj*
nullity nullité[‡] *f*
nullity (eg of legacy) caducité *f*

O

oath serment[‡] *m*
object of no value; worthless security
   non-valeur *f*
object objet[‡] *m*
objection objection[‡] *f*
obligation obligation[‡] *f*; engagement[‡] *m*
obligatory obligatoire[‡] *adj*
oblige (to) obliger *v*

obliged; compelled; required obligé,-e *adj*
obligee; debtor obligé *m*, obligée *f*
obscene pornographique *adj*
obstacle (unexpected); hitch
   empêchement[‡] *m*
occupancy (eg of house) occupation[‡] *f*
occupation occupation[‡] *f*; métier *m*;
   profession *f*; travail[‡] *m*
occupier; occupant occupant[‡] *m*,
   occupante[‡] *f*
of the aforesaid; of the aforementioned
   dudit, desdit(e)s, (see ledit)
offence délit[‡] *m*; infraction[‡] *f*; atteinte[‡] *f*;
   faute[‡] *f*
offence of ordering meal, etc in restaurant
   without being able to pay grivèlerie *f*
offender contrevenant *m*, contrevenante *f*;
   coupable *m,f*
offending contrevenant,-e *adj*
offer offre[‡] *f*
office bureau *m*
office of the mayor mairie *f*
official fonctionnaire[‡] *m,f*
official approval homologation *f*
official document titre[‡] *m*
official notice dénonciation[‡] *f*
official recognition légitimation *f*
official statement (on accident etc) (spoken
   or written) constat[‡] *m*
one making a will testateur *m*, testatrice *f*
opinion avis *m*; opinion *f*
opposability opposabilité *f*
opposing opposant,-e[‡] *adj*
opposition contradiction[‡] *f*; opposition[‡] *f*
option option *f*; faculté[‡] *f*
ordeal épreuve[‡] *f*
order ordre[‡] *m*; arrêté[‡] *m*; ordonnance[‡] *f*;
   prescription *f*
order (to) ordonner *v*
order in council; ordinance décret *m*
order of priority of creditors (in a
   bankruptcy) and sum due to them
   collocation *f*
ordinary; normal ordinaire[‡] *adj*
organic organique *adj*
origin origine[‡] *f*
other party (of transaction) contrepartie *f*
other people; others autrui[‡] *pron*
oust (to) évincer *v*
out-of-court à l'amiable[‡]

outrage outrage[‡] *m*
outstanding pendant,-e *adj*
owing dû, due[‡] *adj*
owing to (events) attendu *prep*
own (possess) propre[‡] *adj*
owner; landowner propriétaire[‡] *m,f*
owner without usufruct nu-propriétaire *m*,
   nue-propriétaire *f*
ownership possession[‡] *f*; propriété[‡] *f*
ownership without usufruct nue-propriété *f*

P

paper; document pièce[‡] *f*
paraph (signature with flourish) paraphe *m*
parcel (of land) parcelle[‡] *f*
pardon (to); absolve (to) absoudre *v*
pardon pardon[‡] *m*
parent parent[‡] *m*, parente[‡] *f*
parking fine; parking ticket
   contravention[‡] *f*
part partie[‡] *f*; rôle[‡] *m*
part (to) séparer *v*
participant intervenant *m*, intervenante *f*
participation participation[‡] *f*
particulars renseignement[‡] *m*
partition (of real property) partage *m*
party (eg to a contract, a dispute) partie[‡] *f*
pass (to) passer[‡] *v*
patent brevet *m*
patentee breveté *m*, brevetée *f*
paternity paternité[‡] *f*
patrimony patrimoine[‡] *m*
pay salaire[‡] *m*
payee (of cheque) bénéficiaire *m,f*
payment règlement *m*
peaceful; calm paisible[‡] *adj*
pen name; stage name pseudonyme *m*
penalty pénalité *f*; peine[‡] *f*; amende *f*;
   astreinte *f*; sanction *f*; dédit *m*
pending pendant,-e *adj*
pension pension[‡] *f*; rente[‡] *f*; retraite[‡] *f*;
perceive (to) percevoir *v*
percentage taux[‡] *m*
perceptible saisissable *adj*
perform (to) (eg contract) exécuter *v*

perjured parjure *adj*
perjurer parjure *m,f*
perjury parjure[‡] *m*; faux serment *m*; faux
   témoignage *m*
permanence inamovibilité *f*
permit-holder licencié *m*, licenciée *f*
permit licence[‡] *f*; permis[‡] *m*; passavant *m*
persistant offender récidiviste *m,f*
person personne[‡] *f*
person entitled (eg to right) titulaire[‡] *m,f*
person guilty of incest incestueux *m*,
   incestueuse *f*
person signing a contract partie *f*
person subject to trial justiciable[‡] *m,f*
person who is of age (18 years or over)
   majeur,-e *m,f*
personal personnel,-elle *adj*
personal property biens[‡] *mpl* personnels;
   mobilier[‡] *m*
pertaining to afférent,-e *adj*
petition demande *f*; pétition *f*; placet *m*;
   requête[‡] *f*
petition for divorce demande *f* en divorce
petitioner (in divorce) demandeur[‡] *m*,
   demanderesse[‡] *f*
pharmacy (technical and legal term for)
   officine *f*
piece of furniture meuble[‡] *m*
piece of writing écrit[‡] *m*
piece pièce[‡] *f*
pilfering chapardage *m*
place (to) (eg seals) apposer *v*
place place[‡] *f*
placing (of an order) passation[‡] *f* (d'une
   commande)
plaintiff plaignant *m*, plaignante *f*;
   demandeur[‡] *m*, demanderesse[‡] *f*;
   poursuivant *m*
plea plaidoyer[‡] *m*; plaidoirie *f*
plead (to) (a cause) plaider[‡] *v*
pledge; collateral security nantissement[‡]
   m; gage[‡] *m*
pledged or pawned article gage[‡] *m*
pledged word foi[‡] *f*
pledging of real estate (eg as security for a
   debt) antichrèse *f*
plot complot *m*
plot (to) comploter *v*
plurality cumul[‡] *m*
point argued (eg of an appeal) branche *f*

project

point of law incident[‡] *m*
poisoning empoisonnement *m*
police; police force police[‡] *f*
policy (assurance, insurance) police[‡] *f*
pollute (to) vicier *v*; polluer *v*
pornographic pornographique *adj*
portion partage *m*
portion of an estate or inheritance
　(additional) préciput[‡] *m*
position place[‡] *f*; qualité[‡] *f*
possession possession[‡] *f*; jouissance[‡] *f*
possession (of fire arms, etc) détention[‡] *f*
possession(s) bien[‡] *m*, biens *mpl*
post-mortem (examination) autopsie *f*
postpone (to) différer *v*; reporter[‡] *v*;
　renvoyer[‡] *v*; surseoir[‡] *v*
postulate (to) postuler *v*
power pouvoir[‡] *m*; puissance[‡] *f*
power of attorney procuration[‡] *f*; mandat[‡]
　m; pouvoir[‡] *m*
powers (of court, etc) compétence[‡] *f*
practise (to) exercer[‡] *v*
preamble exposé *m*
precarious tenure; precarious holding
　précaire *m*
precarious précaire[‡] *adj*
precariousness précarité *f*
preferential right; preference privilège[‡] *m*
pregnancy grossesse[‡] *f*
prejudice préjudice *m*; prévention[‡] *f*
prejudice (to) nuire[‡] *v*
preliminary agreement avant-contrat *m*;
　promesse *f* de vente
premeditated murder assassinat *m*
premeditation préméditation *f*
premises; building local[‡] *m*, locaux[‡] *mpl*;
　immeuble[‡] *m* (see also mur)
premium prime[‡] *f*
prerequisite; condition; preliminary
　préalable[‡] *m*
prescribe (to) prescrire[‡] *v*
prescription ordonnance *f*; prescription[‡] *f*
presence présence[‡] *f*
present présent [‡]*adj*
present again (to) représenter[‡] *v*
present oneself (to) se présenter[‡] *v*
president président[‡] *m*
prestation (of dues, tolls) prestation[‡] *f*
presumed putatif,-ive[‡] *adj*
presumption présomption[‡] *f*

presumptive evidence présomption[‡] *f*
prevention of possession non-jouissance *f*
prevention prévention[‡] *f*
preventively préventivement[‡] *adv*
prima facie evidence commencement *m* de
　preuve
principal (in a transaction) mandant *m*,
　mandante *f*
principal (to a contract) commettant *m*
prior notice préavis *m*
prior; previous; preliminary préalable[‡] *adj*
prison prison *f* (see also maison)
prison cell cellule *f*
prisoner prisonnier *m*, prisonnière *f*
prisoner at the bar accusé *m*, accusée *f*
prisoner's earnings (handed over to him /
　her on release) masse[‡] *f*
private privé,-e[‡] *adj*
private agreement by a document signed
　but not witnessed acte *m* sous seing
　privé
private agreement; private contract
　sous-seing *m*
private individual; private person
　particulier[‡] *m*
private school institution *f*
privilege privilège[‡] *m*
probate (of will) homologation *f*
probation probation[‡] *f*; mise à l'épreuve *f*
probative probant,-e[‡] *adj*
procedure procédure[‡] *f*; démarche[‡] *f*
proceedings procédure[‡] *f*
proceedings (legal) procès[‡] *m*
process server huissier[‡] *m*
procuration procuration[‡] *f*
procurator procureur[‡] *m*
procuring (of prostitute) proxénétisme[‡] *m*
produce or exhibit documents (to) (eg
　before a court) représenter[‡] *v*
production or exhibition (of documents)
　représentation[‡] *f*
profit by (to) bénéficier *v*
profit sharing participation[‡] *f* aux
　bénéfices
profit sharing (scheme) intéressement *m*
profit bénéfice *m*
progress report (eg of building work)
　compte rendu *m*
progress (eg of contract) déroulement[‡] *m*
project; plan; scheme projet[‡] *m*

promise promesse[‡] *f*
promoter; incorporator (company) fondateur[‡] *m*, fondatrice[‡] *f*
pronounce (to) prononcer[‡] *v*
pronouncement prononciation *f*; dispositif *m*; prononcé[‡] *m*
proof épreuve[‡] *f*; constatation *f*; preuve[‡] *f*
property propriété[‡] *f*; avoir *m*; bien[‡] *m*, biens *mpl*; domaine[‡] *m*
property acquired in common by husband and wife acquêt *m*
proportion proportion *f*; quantum[‡] *m*, quanta[‡] *mpl*
proprietor; proprietess propriétaire[‡] *m,f*
proprietorship; ownership propriété[‡] *f*; possession *f*
prosecute (to) poursuivre[‡] *v*
prosecuting (party) poursuivant *m*, poursuivante *f*
prosecution (of crime) vindicte[‡] *f*
prosecution; suing (of a debtor) poursuite[‡] *f*
prosecutor procureur[‡] *m*; poursuivant *m*, poursuivante *f*
prostitution prostitution *f*
protect (to) protéger *v*
protest protêt *m*; protestation *f*
protest (to) protester *v*
prove (to) (eg will) homologuer[‡] *v*
prove innocent (to) innocenter[‡] *v*
provide for (to) prévoir[‡] *v*
provide with a dowry (to) (eg daughter) doter *v*
provision apport[‡] *m*; disposition[‡] *f*; prestation[‡] *f*
provisional provisionnel,-elle[‡] *adj*
proxy procuration[‡] *f*; procureur[‡] *m*; mandataire[‡] *m,f*; mandat[‡] *m*; pouvoir[‡] *m*
public law specialist publiciste *m,f*
public prosecutor's office or department; the prosecution parquet[‡] *m*
publicity publicité[‡] *f*
punishment peine[‡] *f*; sanction *f*
purchase achat[‡] *m*
purchaser acheteur *m*, acheteuse *f*; acquéreur *m*, acquéreuse *f*
purge (to) purger[‡] *v*
purpose objet[‡] *m*; propos[‡] *m*
pursuant to selon *prep*

pursue (to); chase (to) poursuivre[‡] *v*
pursuit poursuite[‡] *f*
purview dispositif *m*
put (to) (eg signature) apposer *v*
put a compulsory purchase order (to) (eg on house, land) exproprier[‡] *v*
put back (to) remettre *v*
put off (to); adjourn (to) remettre *v*; renvoyer *v*
put on (to) revêtir *v*
put out (to) éteindre *v*
putative putatif,-ive[‡] *adj*
pyromaniac pyromane *m,f*

Q

qualification titre[‡] *m*
qualified qualifié,-e[‡] *adj*
quality qualité[‡] *f*
quash (to); set aside (to) (judgement, etc) annuler *v*; casser *v*; infirmer *v*; réformer *v*
quashing infirmatif,-ive *adj*
quashing annulation *f*; infirmation *f*
question (to) interroger *v*
quibbling chicane *f*
quiet paisible[‡] *adj*
quota; portion quote-part *f*; quotes-parts *fpl*; quotité[‡] *f*
quotation devis[‡] *m*

R

raise (to); levy (to) lever[‡] *v*
raise up again (to) relever[‡] *v*
raising; lifting levée[‡] *f*
rank rang[‡] *m*
rape viol[‡] *m*
rate taux[‡] *m*
ratio rapport *m*; taux[‡] *m*
re-establishment redressement[‡] *m*
read, approved and agreed (endorsement with signature on a legal document) lu et approuvé, bon pour accord

real estate biens *mpl* immeubles[‡]; biens *mpl* immobiliers;

reallocate (to) *(fin)* réassigner *v*

reallocation *(fin)* réassignation *f*

reassign (to) (eg right) rétrocéder *v*

reassign (to) réassigner *v*

receipt reçu *m*; quittance *f*

receive (to) (eg pension, salary, rent) percevoir *v*

receive (to) (stolen goods) receler *v*

receiver liquidateur[‡] *m*, liquidatrice[‡] *f*; séquestre[‡] *m*; syndic[‡] *m*

receiver (of stolen goods) receleur *m*, receleuse *f*

receivership redressement *m* judiciaire

receiving and concealing (stolen goods) recel *m*; recelé *m*; recèlement *m*

recision rescision *f*

reclusion réclusion[‡] *f*

recognise (to) reconnaître[‡] *v*

recognise legally (to); legitimate (to) reconnaître[‡] *v*

recognition (eg of a right) reconnaissance[‡] *f*

recognizance; bond; debenture obligation[‡] *f*

reconcile (to) concilier *v*

reconciliation conciliation *f*

reconstruct (to) reconstituer *v*

reconveyance rétrocession *f*

record acte[‡] *m*; casier[‡] *m*

record (eg of evidence) procès-verbal[‡] *m*; procès-verbaux *mpl*

record (to) enregistrer[‡] *v*

recording enregistrement *m*

recount (to); record (to) (facts) relater *v*

recourse recours[‡] *m*

recover possession of (to) ressaisir[‡] *v*

recovery redressement *m*

recovery (eg of debt) recouvrement[‡] *m*

recovery (eg of right) rédemption *f*

rectification rectification *f*

rectify (to) rectifier *v*

recur (to) (disease) récidiver *v*

recurrence (of disease) récidive[‡] *f*

redeem (to) (a mortgage) purger[‡] *v*

redemption (eg of loan) rédemption *f*

redemption (eg of annuity) rachat[‡] *m*

redress réparation[‡] *f*

reduction modération[‡] *f*

reduction; abatement (of tax) dégrèvement *m*

refer to (to) (law, text) invoquer[‡] *v*

referee arbitre *m*

referral renvoi[‡] *m*

reform (to); correct (to) réformer *v*

refund; refunding remboursement *m*

refusal refus[‡] *m*

refuse (to) décliner *v*

regard respect[‡] *m*

regime; system; scheme régime[‡] *m*

register registre[‡] *m* (see also Fichier)

register (to) enregistrer[‡] *v*; inscrire[‡] *v*

register; roll call appel *m*

registered address domicile[‡] *m*

registrar (of commercial court) greffe *m*

registration (of divorce, etc); recording transcription *f*

registration enregistrement[‡] *m*; inscription[‡] *f*; déclaration *f*

registry enregistrement *m*; inscription *f*

registry office bureau *m* de l'état civil

regulation(s) règlement[‡] *m*; réglementation[‡] *f*

reimbursement remboursement *m*

reiterated; repeated itératif,-ive *adj*

relapse into crime récidive[‡] *f*

relate (to) relater *v*

relating to afférent,-e[‡] *adj*

relating to renting of premises locatif[‡], locative[‡] *adj*

relation relation[‡] *f*

relation (blood); relative parent[‡] *m*, parente[‡] *f*

relations (pl); relationship rapport[‡] *m*

release libération[‡] *f*

release (to) libérer[‡] *v*; dessaisir[‡] *v*

release (to) (prisoner) élargir *v*

relegate (to) reléguer *v*

relevant compétent,-e *adj*

reliability sûreté *f*

relief; exemption (from tax) dégrèvement[‡] *m*; agrément *m* fiscal

relinquish (to) (right) délaisser[‡] *v*; se dessaisir *v*

relinquishment or renunciation (of a right) délaissement[‡] *m*; dessaisissement *m*

remark propos[‡] *m*,

remedy réparation[‡] *f*

remission of a sentence pardon[‡] *m*

removability amovibilité *f*
removable amovible *adj*
removal enlèvement[‡] *m*
removal *(med)* prélèvement[‡] *m*
renewal (eg of lease) novation *f*;
  reconduction[‡] *f*; renouvellement *m*
renewal (of a loan) prorogation[‡] *f*
renounce (to); relinquish (to) (eg
  succession) renoncer[‡] *v*; répudier *v*
rent; rental loyer[‡] *m*; rente[‡] *f*;
  redevance[‡] *f*
rental period terme[‡] *m*
renter; hirer locataire *m,f*
renting; tenancy location[‡] *f*
renunciation renonciation[‡] *f*
reoffend (to) récidiver *v*
repayment remboursement *m*
replace (to) remettre *v*
reply (to) répondre[‡] *v*
report or statement (written)
  procès-verbal[‡] *m*
report rapport[‡] *m*; compte rendu[‡] *m*;
  constat[‡] *m*; mémoire[‡] *f*
repossession reprise[‡] *f*; saisie *f*
  immobilière
represent (to) (a client by a lawyer)
  postuler *v*
represent (to) représenter[‡] *v*
representation représentation[‡] *f*
representative interlocuteur[‡] *m*,
  interlocutrice[‡] *f*; mandataire[‡] *m,f*
reprieve sursis[‡] *m*
reproach (to) reprocher[‡] *v*
repudiate (to) nier[‡] *v*; répudier *v*
repudiation désaveu[‡] *m*; rejet *m*;
  répudiation *f*
repurchase rachat[‡] *m*
request; petition demande[‡] *f*; requête[‡] *f*
require (to); claim (to) requérir[‡] *v*
requisition réquisition *f*
rescind (to) annuler *v*; casser *v*; résilier *v*;
  révoquer[‡] *v*
rescindable annulable *adj*
rescinding annulation[‡] *f*; résiliation[‡] *f*
reselling of unlawfully owned goods
  carambouillage *m*; carambouille *f*
reservation réserve[‡] *f*
reserve réserve[‡] *f*
residence résidence[‡] *f*; domicile[‡] *m*;
  demeure *f*

resignation démission[‡] *f*
resolute; determined déliberé,-e *adj*
resolution résolution[‡] *f*
resolutive résolutoire[‡] *adj*
resolve (to) résoudre[‡] *v*
resort; recourse recours[‡] *m*
respect respect[‡] *m*
respondent défendeur *m*, défenderesse *f*;
  intimé *m*, intimée *f*
responsibility responsabilité[‡] *f*
responsible responsable[‡] *adj*
restitution restitution[‡] *f*
restoring réparation[‡] *f*
restrain (to) contraindre *v*
restraint contrainte[‡] *f*; moderation[‡] *f*
restrict to (to) se borner *v* à
restriction (eg of liberty) entrave[‡] *f*
result effet[‡] *m*
resummon (to) réassigner *v*
resummons; fresh summons réassignation *f*
retain (to) retenir[‡] *v*
retainer (lawyer's) honoraires *mpl*
retention rétention[‡] *f*
retirement (from work) retraite[‡] *f*
retract (to) rétracter[‡] *v*
retraction; disavowal désaveu[‡] *m*;
  rétractation *f*
retroactive rétroactif,-ive *adj*
retroactively rétroactivement *adv*
retrocede (to) rétrocéder *v*
retrocedence; retrocession rétrocession *f*
retrospective rétroactif,-ive *adj*
retrospectively rétroactivement *adv*
return relevé[‡] *m*; renvoi[‡] *m*
return (to) retourner[‡] *v*; renvoyer[‡] *v*
return retour[‡] *m*
revenue revenu[‡] *m*
reversal; reversing; quashing; setting aside
  (of sentence, will, etc) cassation *f*
reverse (to); quash (to) annuler *v*;
  réformer *v*
reversible réversible *adj*
reversion réversion[‡] *f*
reversion (eg of an inheritance) retour[‡] *m*
revertible (eg succession) réversible *adj*
revocable rétractable *adj*
revocable at pleasure (office) amovible *adj*
revocation révocation[‡] *f*
revocatory révocatoire[‡] *adj*
revoke (to) révoquer[‡] *v*

setting aside

rider; additional clause avenant *m*
right of inheritance hérédité *f*
right of reemption réméré[‡] *m*
right droit[‡] *m*
right; option faculté[‡] *f*; option *f*
right to represent (a client by a lawyer)
   postulation *f*
right to use and enjoy the benefits of
   another's property usufruit
rightful claimant or owner ayant-droit *m*;
   ayants-droit *mpl*
rightfully légitimement *adv*
riot émeute *f*
risk risque *m*
rogatory (commission) rogatoire *adj*
role rôle[‡] *m*
roll; list rôle[‡] *m*
room local *m*, locaux *mpl*; pièce[‡] *f*;
   chambre *f*
rough draft; preliminary version projet[‡] *m*;
   avant-projet *m*; avant-projets *mpl*
row rang[‡] *m*
royalty (author's) honoraires *mpl*
rule règle[‡] *f*
rules réglementation *f*
ruling décision[‡] *f*; ordonnance *f*; arrêt
run again (to) recourir[‡] *v*
rung (of ladder) barreau *m*
rupture rupture[‡] *f*

S

safeguard; safe keeping sauvegarde[‡] *f*
safety securité[‡] *f*; sûreté[‡] *f*
salaried employee salarié *m*, salariée *f*
salary salaire[‡] *m*
sale vente[‡] *f*
sale by auction in one lot of property held
   in indivision licitation *f*
save sauf[‡] *prep*
schedule (to a contract) annexe *f*
schedule of conditions cahier *m* des
   charges
scrounging chapardage *m*
seal (official) scellé[‡] *m*
seal, seals sceau *m*, sceaux *mpl*

search (house) perquisition *f*
seat siege *m*
seclusion; illegal restraint séquestration *f*
second offence; subsequent offence
   récidive[‡] *f*
secure (to) (eg a creditor) nantir[‡] *v*
security caution[‡] *f*; gage[‡] *m*; nantissement[‡] *m*; garantie *f*; securité[‡] *f*
seek (to); hunt for (to) rechercher *v*
seisin; legal possession of a freehold estate
   saisine *f*
seizable; distrainable saisissable *adj*
seize (to) (goods, property) confisquer *v*;
   saisir[‡] *v*
seize again (to) ressaisir *v*
seizure (court order) saisie[‡] *f*
seizure mainmise *f*
sell off (to) liquider[‡] *v*
seller vendeur *m*, vendeuse *f*, venderesse *f*
send back (to); return (to) renvoyer[‡] *v*
sending back renvoi[‡] *m*
sending envoi[‡] *m*
senior police officer officier *m* de police
   judiciaire (OPJ)
sentence condamnation[‡] *f*; peine[‡] *f*;
   sentence[‡] *f*; jugement[‡] *m*
sentence (to) condamner[‡] *v*
separate séparé,-e *adj*
separate (to) (eg husband and wife)
   séparer *v*
separate valuation (of chattels or parts of
   an estate) ventilation *f*
separated (eg persons) séparé,-e *adj*
separation séparation[‡3] *f*
sequestration (of property) séquestre[‡] *m*;
   séquestration *f*
sequestrator séquestre[‡] *m*
serve (to) délivrer *v*
serve a writ (to) assigner *v*
serve notice of (to); notify (to) signifier[‡] *v*
serving of a writ, summons or process
   assignation[‡] *f*
session; sitting (of officials) session *f*;
   vacation *f*
set down (to) déposer *v*
set forth (to) (facts) articuler *v*
set off (to) (eg debts); clear (to) (cheques)
   compenser *v*
setting aside (eg will); voidance;
   cancellation (eg contract) annulation *f*

setting forth (facts) articulation *f*
setting-up constitution[‡] *f*
settle (to) (eg succession, debt, account)
  liquider[‡] *v*; régler *v*; constituer[‡] *v*
settlement accord *m*; donation *f*;
  arrangement *m*; transaction *f*;
  règlement[‡] *m*
settlement per contra compensation *f*
settlor constituant *m*
shape forme[‡] *f*
share quotité *f*; partage[‡] *m*; quote-part *f*;
  quotes-parts *fpl*; quotité[‡] *f*
share of estate lot *m*
sharing participation[‡] *f*
sharing out répartition[‡] *f*
shield (to) protéger *v*; soustraire[‡] *v*
sickness maladie[‡] *f*
sight vu[‡] *m*
sign (to) signer *v*; parapher *v*
sign one's initials on (to) parapher *v*
signature; signing signature[‡] *f*
significance signification[‡] *f*
signify (to) signifier[‡] *v*
signing acceptation *f*; signature *f*;
  passation[‡] *f*
simpleton innocent,-e *adj*; innocent *m*,
  innocente *f*
simulate (to) simuler[‡] *v*
skilled qualifié,-e[‡] *adj*
slander (to) diffamer *v*
slander diffamation[‡] *f*; calomnie *f*
slandering (verbal); libelling (written)
  diffamation *f*
slanderous diffamatoire *adj*
slang jargon[‡] *m*; argot *m*
society société[‡] *f*; association *f*
soliciting (by prostitute) racolage *m*
solicitor avocat *m*; avocate *f*; avoué *m*;
  notaire *m*
solidarity solidarité *f*
soluble (eg problem) soluble *adj*
solution résolution[‡] *f*
solve (to) résoudre *v*
source origine[‡] *f*
speaker; person interlocuteur[‡] *m*,
  interlocutrice[‡] *f*
specification spécification *f*; cahier *m* des
  charges; devis[‡] *m*
specified item stipulation[‡] *f*; prescription[‡] *f*

specify (to); state precisely (to); give
  precise details (to) préciser[‡] *v*
speech for the defence plaidoirie *f*;
  plaidoyer[‡] *m*
splitting séparation[‡] *f*
spouse époux[‡] *m*, épouse[‡] *f*; conjoint[‡] *m*,
  conjointe *f*
spread (abroad) (to) diffuser *v*
spying espionnage[‡] *m*
squatting occupation *f* de fait de la maison
  d'autrui
stamped timbré,-e *adj*
stand down (to) désister (se) *v*
stand up for (to) défendre *v*
standing order (bank) prélèvement[‡] *m*
state (to) décliner *v*
state (fact) clearly (to) articuler *v*
state precisely (to) préciser[‡] *v*
state; condition état[‡] *m*
statement compte *m*; dire[‡] *m*; exposé[‡] *m*;
  relevé[‡] *m*; énoncé *m*; état *m*
statement (sworn) déposition[‡] *f*
statement of accounts bilan[‡] *m*
statement of case; report mémoire[‡] *f*
statute law juridisprudence *f*
statute of limitations prescription[‡] *f*
statutory legal,-e *adj*
stay (to) (eg proceedings) surseoir[‡] *v*
stay of proceedings suspension[‡] *f*
stealing; swindling filouterie *f*
step; procedure démarche[‡] *f*
still dormant,-e *adj*
stimulation excitation *f*
stipulate (to) prescrire[‡] *v*; stipuler *v*;
  préciser *v*
stipulation condition[‡] *f*; stipulation[‡] *f*;
  disposition[‡] *f*
stocklist inventaire[‡] *m*
stop (to) arrêter *v*; cesser[‡] *v*
strength puissance[‡] *f*; vigueur[‡] *f*
strike grève[‡] *f*
striker gréviste *m,f*
study (to) considérer *v*
subcontract (to) marchander *v*;
  sous-traiter *v*
subcontractor sous-traitant *m*
subcontractor (of labour) marchandeur *m*,
  marchandeuse *f*
subject matter matière[‡] *f*
subject to judgement in court jugeable[‡] *adj*

subject to seizure saisissable *adj*
subject; liable assujetti *adj*
submission of a case to the court saisine *f*
submit (to); refer (to) (case to court)
  déférer‡ *v*
suborn (to) suborner *v*
subornation subornation‡ *f*
subpoena mandement *m*; assignation *f* à
  comparaître
subpoena someone (to) ajourner *v*;
  assigner *v* à comparaître
subrogate (to) subroger *v*
subrogated subrogé,-e *adj*
subrogation; substitution subrogation‡ *f*
subscription cotisation *f*
subsequent subséquent,-e *adj*
subsequent to (à) postérieur *adj*
subsequently subséquemment *adv*
subsidy prime‡ *f*; subvention‡ *f*
substitute (to) subroger *v*
substitution (of a new obligation for a
  previous one) novation *f*
subtract (to) soustraire‡ *v*
subvention subvention‡ *f*
succeed (to) hériter‡ *v*; succéder à *v*
succeed jointly (to) copartager *v* (une
  succession)
succession succession‡ *f*; hoirie *f*
sue (to) actionner *v*
suicide suicide‡ *m*
suing (of a debtor) poursuite *f*
suit (to) convenir *v*
suit; lawsuit cause‡ *f*; procès *m*
suited; suitable apte *adj*
sully (to); taint (to); blemish (to)
  entacher‡ *v*
sum somme‡ *f*
sum paid secretly to the vendor, in addition
  to the declared price dessous-de-table *m*
sum up (to) résumer *v*
summarize (to) résumer *v*
summary procedure référé‡ *m*
summary; summing-up résumé‡ *m*
summon (to) intimer‡ *v*; sommer‡ *v*
summon (to); subpoena (to) (a witness)
  citer *v*; assigner *v*; ajourner *v*
summons (before an appeal court)
  intimation‡ *f*
summons or formal notice (to do
  something) mise *f* en demeure;

commandement *m*; convocation *f*;
  sommation‡ *f*; citation‡ *f*
support (to) avaliser *v*
supposed censé *adj*
surety caution‡ *f*
surplus excès‡ *m*
surrender (of insurance policy) rachat‡ *m*
surrender (to) (right) céder‡ *v*
surrogate subrogé,-e‡ *adj*
surrogate mother mère *f* porteuse
surveillance surveillance *f*
survey levé‡ *m*; enquête *f*; expertise‡ *f*
surviving survivant,-e *adj*
survivor survivant *m*, survivante *f*
suspect suspect *m*
suspend (to) suspendre *v*
suspended or deferred sentence (with a)
  sursitaire *adj*
suspended sentence sursis‡ *m*
suspension exclusion *f*; suspension‡ *f*
suspensive suspensif,-ive *adj*
suspicious; suspect suspect *adj*
swindle; swindling; fraud escroquerie‡ *f*;
  filouterie *f*
swindle (to) escroquer *v*
switching commutation *f*
syndic syndic‡ *m*
syndicate syndicat‡ *m*
system régime‡ *m*

T

tacit tacite‡ *adj*
tailoring to individual requirements (eg
  sentencing) individualisation *f*
take back (to) reporter‡ *v*
take cognizance of (to) connaître de‡ *v*
take into custody (to) saisir‡ *v*
take issue (to); protest (to) contester *v*
take on (to); sign on (to) (workmen etc)
  embaucher *v*
take up (to); exercise (to) (eg option)
  lever‡ *v*
taken pris,-e‡ *adj*
takeover mainmise *f*
tax impôt‡ *m*; taxe‡ *f*

tax (to) taxer *v*
tax liability; taxation; tax rate impôt[‡] *m*
tax system; taxation system fiscalité[‡] *f*
taxation taxe[‡] *f*
teach (to); instruct (to) instruire *v*
telephone tapping écoute *f* téléphonique
tenancy agreement bail *m*; baux *mpl*
tenant locataire[‡] *m,f*; preneur *m*,
  preneuse *f*
tenant farming fermage *m*
tenant for life usufruitier *m*, usufruitière *f*
tenant in common indivisaire *m,f*
tenure tenure[‡] *f*; jouissance[‡] *f*
term (at law courts) session *f*
term clause *f*; condition[‡] *f*; terme[‡] *m*
terminate (to) résilier[‡] *v*
termination résiliation[‡] *f*
terrorism terrorisme *m*
test essai[‡] *m*
testament; will testament *m*
testator testateur *m*, testatrice *f*
testify (to) déposer[‡] *v*; témoigner[‡] *v*
testimony déposition[‡] *f*; témoignage[‡] *m*
the accused inculpé *m*, inculpée *f* (l')
the aforementioned ledit *m*; ladite *f*;
  lesdit(e)s *pl adj* (see also audit, dudit)
the aforesaid (in legal documents) ledit *m*;
  ladite *f*; lesdit(e)s *pl,adj*
the one, those *pl*, he, she icelui, icelle,
  iceux, icelles *pron* (= celui-ci, celle-ci,
  ceux-ci, celles-ci)
theft vol[‡] *m*; chapardage *m*
thing understood sous-entendu *m*
third party tiers[‡] (m,inv); tiers, tierce *adj*
threat menace[‡] *f*
threatening (letter) comminatoire *adj*
three-year period triennat *m*
tie (to) lier *v*
tie up (to) (capital) immobiliser *v*
tied; assessed assujetti *adj*
time heure[‡] *f*; terme[‡] *f*
time (to) minuter[‡] *v*
time-limit; extension of time délai[‡] *m*
title habilité[‡] *f*; titre[‡] *m*; droit[‡] *m*
title (of address given to lawyers, notaires,
  etc) maître[‡] *m*
titular titulaire[‡] *adj*
to the aforesaid; to the aforementioned
  (also at, in, on, from) audit, auxdit(e)s
  (see ledit[‡])

tontine tontine[‡] *f*
tort injure[‡] *f*; préjudice[‡] *m*; acte *m*
  délictuel
tortious; prejudicial dommageable *adj*
total amount montant[‡] *m*
town hall mairie *f*
town planning urbanisme[‡] *m*
trade union syndicat[‡] *m*
tradition tradition *f*
traffic trafic[‡] *m*
trafficking trafic[‡] *m*
training formation[‡] *f*
transaction transaction *f*
transactional transactionnel,-elle[‡] *adj*
transcription; transcribing transcription *f*
transfer (eg of ownership, property)
  mutation[‡] *f* (see also remise)
transfer; conveyance (eg right, property)
  translation *f*; cession[‡] *f*
transfer (to) (eg property, rights) aliéner *v*;
  céder[‡] *v*
transferability cessibiité *f*
transferable cessible *adj*
transferee cessionnaire *m*
transferor cédant *m*, cédante *f*
transformation mutation[‡] *f*
transire (customs permit) passavant *m*
translate (to) traduire *v*
translation traduction *f* (text); translation *f*
  (transfer)
transmission (of property, etc) dévolution *f*
transport transport[‡] *m*
transport (to) transporter[‡] *v*
traverse dénégation[‡] *f*
treasure; treasure trove trésor[‡] *m*
treasury trésor[‡] *m*
trial essai[‡] *m*; procès[‡] *m*; jugement[‡] *m*
trouble trouble[‡] *m*
trust fidéicommis[‡] *m*
trustee fiduciaire[‡] *m*; consignataire *m*;
  fidéicommissaire *m*; syndic[‡] *m*;
  dépositaire *m,f*
trusteeship fidéicommis[‡] *m*;
  fidéicommissariat *m*
trusteeship (in bankruptcy) syndicat[‡] *m*
truth vérité *f*
try (to) juger[‡] *v*
turn off (to); switch off (to) éteindre *v*
turn over / up / down / back (to)
  retourner[‡] *v*

tutelage tutelle[‡] *f*
tutelary tutélaire[‡] *adj*

U

unauthorised assumption (of a right, qualificaton, etc) usurpation *f*
uncertainty of tenure (of office) amovibilité *f*
undeniable irréfragable *adj*
under; by virtue of selon *prep*; en vertu[‡] *f* de
undercover payment dessous-de-table *m*
undersigned (the) soussigné[‡] *m*, soussignée[‡] *f*; also *adj*
understanding entente[‡] *f*
undertake (to) engager[‡] *v*
undertaking to pay; promissory note *(com)* promesse[‡] *f*
underwriter assureur *m*
undeserving indigne[‡] *adj*
undivided indivis,-e[‡] *adj*
unemployed person chômeur *m*, chômeuse *f*
unemployment chômage[‡] *m*
uneven irrégulier,-ière[‡] *adj*
unfitness inaptitude *f*
unfitted; incapable inhabile[‡] *adj*
unilateral unilatéral,-e *adj*
unlawful illégal,-e *adj*
unless sauf[‡] *prep*
unobserved inobservé,-e *adj*
unoccupied (eg house) vacant,-e[‡] *adj*
unrepealable inabrogeable *adj*
unrestricted libre[‡] *adj*
unrolling; unwinding déroulement *m*
unsuitability inaptitude *f*
untroubled paisible[‡] *adj*
untrue faux[‡], fausse[‡] *adj*
unwarranted interference (in an affair) immixtion[‡] *f*
upholder of the law justicier *m*, justicière *f*
uproar; racket tapage[‡] *m*
urgent; imperative impératif,-ve *adj*; urgent,-e *adj*
use usage[‡] *m*

use; possession of; tenure jouissance[‡] *f*
using usage[‡] *m*; mise *f* en œuvre
usufruct usufruit[‡] *m*
usufructuary usufruitier *m*, usufruitière *f*; (also *adj*)
usurp (to) usurper[‡] *v*
usurpation usurpation *f*
usurpatory usurpatoire[‡] *adj*

V

vacant vacant,-e[‡] *adj*
vacation; recess (of law courts) vacation *f*
vagrancy vagabondage *m*
valid valide[‡] *adj*; valable[‡] *adj*
validity valeur[‡] *f*; validité[‡] *f*
validly validement *adv*
valuation (of investments, securities, etc) inventaire[‡] *m*
value valeur[‡] *f*
value separately (to) (chattels or parts of an estate) ventiler *v*
vendee acheteur *m*, acheteuse *f*; acquéreur *m*, acquéreuse *f*
vendor or buyer (when represented by an agent) commettant *m*
vendor; seller vendeur[‡] *m*, vendeuse[‡] *f*; venderesse[‡] *f*
ventilate (to) ventiler *v*
ventilation ventilation *f*
verdict verdict[‡] *m*
verification constatation[‡] *f*; vérification *f*
verify (to) constater *v*; vérifier *v*
vest (to) investir[‡] *v*
vice; corruption vice[‡] *m*
victim victime[‡] *f*
viduity viduité *f*
vigour vigueur[‡] *f*
violation violation[‡] *f*
violence violence[‡] *f*
virtue vertu[‡] *f*
visit; visiting visite[‡] *f*
vitiate (to) entacher[‡] *v*; vicier *v*
voidable annulable *adj*; résoluble *adj*
voluntarily volontairement *adv*
vouch for (to) attester *v*

WXYZ

wage-earner salarié *m*, salariée *f*
wages gain[‡] *m*; salaire[‡] *m*
waiting period délai[‡] *m*
waive (to) renoncer *v*
waiver (of claim) désistement *m*;
  renonciation [‡]*f*
wall mur[‡] *m*
ward pupille[‡] *m,f*
wardship tutelle[‡] *m*
warning sommation[‡] *f*
warning (eg of dismissal) avertissement *m*
warrant brevet *m*; certificat *m*
warrant of arrest décret *m*; mandat *m*
  d'arrêt
warrant (to) garantir[‡] *v*
warranty garantie[‡] *f*
way; road voie[‡] *f*
well and truly bel et bien *adv*
well of court parquet[‡] *m*
well-founded fondé,-e[‡] *adj*; fondé *m* de
  pouvoir
whether... or... soit... soit... *(conj)*
widen (to); broaden (to); enlarge (to)
  élargir *v*
widowed man, widower veuf *m*
widowed woman; widow veuve *f*
widowerhood (man) viduité[‡] *f*
widowhood (woman) viduité[‡] *f*
wife femme *f*; épouse *f*
wilful damage bris *m*
will testament[‡] *m*; volonté *f*
winding-up (eg of a company) dissolution *f*
winning gagnant,-e[‡] *adj*
withdraw (to) (eg statement) rétracter[‡] *v*
withdraw (to) se désister[‡] *v*; renoncer *v*
withdrawal mainlevée[‡] *f*; retrait[‡] *m*;
  rétractation *f*
withdrawal (of suit, defence, etc)
  désistement *m*
witness témoin[‡] *m*
witness box banc *m* des témoins; barre *f*
  (des témoins)
witness statement témoignage *m*
witnessing certification *f*
woman femme[‡] *f*

word(s) written over others (as correction,
  insertion or over erasure) surcharge *f*
wording rédaction[‡] *f*; énoncé[‡] *m*
work travail[‡] *m*; travaux[‡] *mpl*
worker travailleur[‡] *m*, travailleuse[‡] *f*
worsening aggravation *f*
wreck; stray épave *f*
writ of execution exécutoire[‡] *m*
writ of summons (from one counsel to
  another) avenir *m*
writ of summons or subpoena assignation *f*
writ; process; summons; notice exploit[‡] *m*
write down (to) inscrire[‡] *v*
written exam or paper écrit[‡] *m*
wrong (to) léser[‡] *v*
wrong tort[‡] *m*; préjudice[‡] *m*; lésion *f*
wrongful abusif,-ive[‡] *adj*; dommageable
  adj; illicite[‡] *adj*

year année *f*

HADLEY PAGER INFO PUBLICATIONS
French-English, English-French

CONCISE DICTIONARY OF HOUSE BUILDING TERMS
(Arranged by Trades)

Paperback, 1994, 240 pages, 210 x 148 mm
ISBN 1-872739-02-4   Price: £25.00
- Entirely new compilation
- Divided into 14 Sections: Architecte, Fondations, Maçon, Charpentier et Menuisier, Bois et Placages, Couvreur, Quincaillier, Métaux, Plombier, Vitrier, Électricien, Plâtrier, Peintre-Décorateur, Couleurs
- Over 10,000 terms in each language

GLOSSARY OF HOUSE PURCHASE AND RENOVATION TERMS

Paperback, 3rd edition, 1996, 52 pages, 210 x 148 mm
ISBN 1-872739-04-0   Price: £7.50
- Provides over 1900 French words and phrases used by estate agents, notaires, mortgage lenders, builders, decorators, etc.

HADLEY'S CONVERSATIONAL FRENCH PHRASE BOOK

Paperback, 1997, 256 pages, 148 x 105 mm
ISBN 1-872739-05-9   Price: £5.95
- Over 2000 French phrases with English equivalents
- Over 2000 English phrases with French equivalents
- Eleven conversational topic vocabularies
- Aide-memoire key word dictionary

GLOSSARY OF GARDENING AND HORTICULTURAL TERMS

Paperback, 1998, 44 pages, 210 x 148 mm
ISBN 1-872739-06-7   Price: £8.50
- The glossary includes around 1500 gardening and horticultural terms
- The glossary matches up the familiar French and English names of pot and garden flowering plants and shrubs which are not readily available.

The above publications are available through good booksellers or can be ordered directly from Hadley Pager Info by sending a cheque to cover the price (postage is free within the UK, add 10% if outside the UK) to Hadley Pager Info, Surrey House, 114 Tilt Road, Cobham, Surrey, KT11 3JH, England. Latest Publication List available on request.